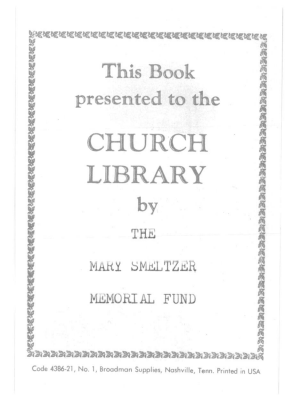

Fear in Algeria

Fear in Algeria

Marian Hostetler

Illustrated by
James Converse

HERALD PRESS
Scottdale, Pennsylvania
Kitchener, Ontario
1979

Library of Congress Cataloging in Publication Data

Hostetler, Marian, 1932-
    Fear in Algeria.

    SUMMARY: When the 14-year-old daughter of Christian
missionaries visits Algeria, her association with those
of her faith leads her to unexpected adventure.
    [1. Christian life—Fiction. 2. Algeria—Fiction]
I. Converse, James. II. Title.
PZ7.H8112Fe   [Fic]   79-18132
ISBN 0-8361-1904-5
ISBN 0-8361-1905-3 pbk.

FEAR IN ALGERIA
Copyright © 1979 by Herald Press, Scottdale, Pa. 15683
    Published simultaneously in Canada by Herald Press,
    Kitchener, Ont. N2G 4M5
Library of Congress Catalog Card Number: 79-18132
International Standard Book Numbers:
    0-8361-1904-5 (hardcover)
    0-8361-1905-3 (softcover)
Printed in the United States of America
Design: Alice B. Shetler

15 14 13 12 11 10 9 8 7 6 5 4 3 2 1

To all the girls at
Henchir Toumghani
who taught me while
I was trying to
teach them.

My thanks to Mary Ellen Shoup, Ann McGovern, and my editor, Paul M. Schrock, for their careful reading of the manuscript and for their helpful suggestions.

I suppose you could say I was going home. Only I didn't remember having been there before. If this sounds confusing, I'll try to explain. I was born in Algeria when my parents were working in North Africa for Church Overseas Aid. But thirteen years ago, when I was just over a year old, we had left there and returned to the United States.

Well, I know a lot about Algeria, of course. My parents still talk about it often. Then, too, I've met some of their friends from those days who knew me as a tiny baby. They always exclaim when we see them, "My, how you've grown!" Also, I've probably seen my folks' slides of Algeria at least a hundred times.

They even gave me an Algerian name—Zina (pronounced *zee-na* and meaning "beautiful"). Arabic is the national language there, so they also taught me a few Arabic phrases and how to write the Arabic alphabet. Many Algerians also speak French, and since I've been studying French this year in school, I thought I was pretty well prepared for my visit.

I was wrong, though. Seeing something firsthand isn't the same as hearing about it or looking at pictures. So I know that when I write down for you what happened to me there and what I saw, it won't be the same for you as it was for me. Still, I've read stories which seemed to carry me to another time, another place. That's what I want to do for you. So please come with me—I want to take you along when I go "home."

My first inkling of something unusual was at the supper table one cold January evening. I had finally been to school again following three days off because of a blizzard. The weather had been so bad no mail had been delivered for several days. So maybe the letter from Lillian had been lying around the post office awhile before arriving at our house that day.

I suppose Mother had that extra sparkle in her eyes she always has when something exciting is going to happen, but this time I didn't notice. I was too busy thinking about all the homework the teachers had loaded on us because of the missed days. I found out later that, earlier in the afternoon, she had called Dad at the bookstore where he works so they could discuss the situation.

My first clue came when Mother said, "You remember Lillian Thomas, don't you, Zene?" (They often call me "Zene" for short.)

I thought a bit. "Oh, sure—she's the old lady who

stopped to see us last summer on her way back to Algeria. She's been teaching school there a long time—since before you were there."

Dad sighed, then half laughed. "I guess I once considered forty to be old, too, but no more—no more. Otherwise, you're right on target."

"The thing is, Zene," Mother went on, "we got a letter from Lil today, and she's invited you to come to Algeria for a visit during your spring vacation. The problem is whether we have the money to get you there. She thinks you ought to see the country where you were born, and so do we. What do you think?"

"Oh, I'd love it! That sounds terribly exciting!" I burst out. Visions of camels, Sahara Desert sands, veiled women, and the blue Mediterranean Sea flashed into my mind, like the slides of them I'd so often seen flashing onto the screen. Then I remembered that Mother had said money was a problem. And the dream faded.

"But—how much does it cost?" I said in a wavering voice.

"I've checked with the travel agent," Dad said. "A direct round-trip flight from Chicago isn't as much as I thought it might be. If we get reservations 45 days ahead and you stay two weeks, it's quite a bit less than the regular fare. We've decided we can scrape together half the cost, if you're willing to pay the rest from the college money Grandma Johnson put in the bank for you. I called her this afternoon, and she doesn't mind if you use it for that—if that's what you want to do."

I didn't hesitate. "That's what I want to do."

Sometimes I had gotten tired of them talking about Algeria, especially when their friends from Algeria were around. It was "Algeria this" and "Algeria that" and "when we were in Algeria something else." I think I was a little jealous. Now the jealousy had vanished. In fact, I probably began to bore the kids at school with my own "Algeria this" and "Algeria that." But I couldn't help it. I was so excited about going.

We applied for my passport right away. A few weeks later we got it. But that didn't make it sure that I could go. It was really only the United States government's permit for me to travel to other countries. I also needed a visa stamped in it from the Algerian government giving me permission to enter their country, or I couldn't go.

This part seemed to take forever. The travel agent had sent my passport and request for a visa to the Algerian consulate office in Washington, D.C. We waited and waited, but no answer came. The travel agent called the consulate several times. They didn't say yes or no, but said they needed to wait until permission came from Algiers, the capital.

"I wonder if she isn't getting the visa because she was born there?" Mother finally asked Dad.

"Oh, I doubt it. If anything, that should make it easier for her to get a visa."

"I'm not sure about that. Remember, several years after we returned to the States, when we wanted to go to Algeria for a visit they wouldn't give us a visa."

"Oh, that's right, and we never did know why.

10

But that was years ago. There shouldn't be any problem for Zina now."

Then it was only a week until I would leave—and still no visa. I was nearly convinced that I wouldn't be able to go after all, and we would have to cancel the trip, when the travel agency phoned me to pick up my passport. It had come back with the visa stamped in it!

The last few days were a mad rush. I had to get a doctor's appointment for a typhoid shot and a smallpox vaccination. The doctor also gave me some pills to take so that I wouldn't get malaria. Then there were the last-minute things we needed to buy for the trip. And we had to write Lillian to say for sure I was coming. Mother had written her before so she'd know what plane to meet, but we hadn't been sure then if I could actually go.

Now that it was time to leave, I suddenly wasn't so sure I really wanted to go.

I had flown a couple of times before, but never by myself, never for such a distance, and never in a jumbo jet. I could have gone by plane from South Bend, Indiana, where we live, to O'Hare International Airport in Chicago. Mother and Dad decided to drive me there, though. I was glad they had, especially when I saw how huge the airport was.

And the noise and confusion inside the terminal was worse. People rushed around madly. Loudspeakers announced flights and paged passengers. Blinking lights on big announcement boards and on small TV screens showed flight times and the gates the planes were leaving from. People waited impatiently to check their baggage in and to receive their seat assignments. Some airline workers were trying to help passengers find lost baggage. Others were trying to help frantic customers who missed their planes get other flights.

In spite of all this we finally managed to find Trans American Lines. The man behind the counter checked my ticket, put a tag on my suitcase, and threw it onto a moving belt. The belt whisked it through some folding doors and out of sight.

Mother and Dad went with me to the corridor leading to my gate, Gate G, but there we had to say goodbye. Only those with tickets could go on through the security check and to the waiting rooms. I sort of hated to leave them and go on alone, but I made myself kiss them goodbye, and started down the corridor.

Then I turned and called, "Oh river!" (The French word for goodbye is *au revoir*, pronounced oh-re-vwar). This was my attempt at being funny. Maybe I should explain that some people think I have a good sense of humor. So when I'm nervous or scared, I try to be funny. But sometimes, like this time, what comes out is not all that clever.

Bad joke or not, I had to move along. My parents had explained to me what would be happening next, so I wasn't surprised when I was asked to set my shoulder bag on a moving belt. I watched it travel through a metal-detecting device. Then I had to step through a sort of open doorway metal-detector which checked to make sure I wasn't carrying any hidden weapons. My bag and I both passed our tests, so we went on to a room already nearly full of people waiting for my flight.

I didn't know anyone, so I couldn't make any funny remarks—except to myself, and I was too nervous to be able to amuse myself. Before long, the plane was ready for boarding, and we lined up and filed through a door, down a short hallway, and onto the plane. Once inside, I could see why these 747s are called jumbo jets. It was wide—three sections with three seats in each section. I was disappointed to be in the middle part, because I wouldn't be able to see out the windows.

I won't bore you with all the details of the trip—only that I enjoyed the meals—snack, dinner, and breakfast. I liked the food, as well as the neat way nearly everything came in little packages on the tray. I didn't watch the movie. It cost $2.50 for the little earphones to listen to the sound that went with the film. And it wasn't one I was interested in. I read a book instead, a mystery by Agatha Christie, one of my favorite authors.

The plane wasn't full, so I could use two seats to curl up in. Even so, I didn't sleep much. Perhaps I was too excited—and worried. I began to wonder what I would do if Lillian wasn't there to meet me. I was sure my few words of French and my knowing how to say "thank you" in Arabic wouldn't help much.

We passed through several time zones as we headed east, chasing after the sun. This made the night only half as long as usual. In the morning we landed at Madrid, Spain. But I never saw Madrid, nor Spain—nothing but the airport as I hurried to change planes.

The Madrid to Algiers plane was smaller. I barely had time to get acquainted with it till Spain

I didn't see Madrid—nothing but the airport as I hurried to change planes.

14

was left behind and the Mediterranean Sea was spread out under us. This time I had a window seat and could see that blue, blue sea sparkling below.

Before long, brown and gray smudges appeared on the horizon ahead. Soon I could see that the smudges were really rugged mountains. The coast of North Africa was looming across the horizon. And beyond those ridges, stretching on and on to the south for five thousand miles, was the vast continent of Africa.

Then we began our descent to Algiers. Even from the air I could tell I was coming to a place completely different from what I'd known before in Indiana or in the other places I'd traveled in the United States. I caught glimpses of red-tile-roofed farm buildings, of palm trees, and even of a camel strolling down a highway. And everything I saw glowed in bright colors, lit by the brilliant African sun and the cloudless blue sky.

What I saw was beautiful, but strange and different. The butterflies in my stomach really started fluttering.

We had arrived at *Maison Blanche* (White House), the Algiers airport. When I stepped from the plane, the colors were more brilliant, the sun and sky brighter than I'd thought. It was because I was now seeing them for real rather than through the not-too-clean plane windows.

Then it was down the steps of the plane and onto a bus for the short drive to the terminal. As we went up the sidewalk toward the white stucco building, gracefully arching palms and flowering hedges welcomed us.

Once inside, when I saw that the only people in sight were passengers and officials, my fear returned. I hadn't realized that those who came to meet the planes would be kept separate from the passengers until our passports had been checked. I was on my own, so I would just have to watch the people ahead of me and do what they did.

Slowly the line moved along. And then it was my turn. Timidly, I placed my passport in front of the policeman behind the glass window, just as I had seen the person ahead of me do. He looked at my picture on the passport, at me, at my visa, and then glanced over the card I'd been asked to fill out on the plane before we landed. It told such things as why I was coming and where I was staying.

"You are young to be alone, isn't it?" he asked me in accented, incorrect English.

"My friend is meeting me here," I said, adding in my mind, "I hope."

He stamped my passport. "Enjoy your stay," he said, and motioned me on. But that wasn't the end. The line continued. At the next stop I had to fill out papers saying how much and what kind of money I was bringing into the country. I didn't have much, only a few travelers' checks. That was all I needed (so I thought), since I would be with Lillian all of the time and not have many expenses.

But still we had not finished. Next I had to find my suitcase (by that time they had all been taken off the plane and were stacked nearby, waiting to be claimed). I spotted mine and managed to pull it out from underneath some others. Then I got in line again.

When it was my turn, I had to unlock my suitcase while a customs official looked through my things. I wasn't sure what they were searching for, but I didn't have anything except my clothes and some gifts of food Mother and Dad had sent along for Lillian—things like canned corn and ham and Jello that she liked, but which are hard to get here. And I had some little gifts for some friends of my parents, whom I was supposed to visit. The man raised his eyebrows at the food items, but they mustn't have been illegal, because he okayed my suitcase and motioned me to go on.

Now I was where I could see the people who were waiting for the passengers. They were clustered behind a sort of fence, eager eyes searching for their relatives or friends. My eyes searched too, but I didn't see Lillian. Maybe she was behind someone. She wasn't very tall and might be out of sight.

I made my way through the gate and then through the waiting throng. Now I was in the clear—and I still hadn't seen Lillian. Perhaps she'd wanted to stay away from the crowd and was waiting further back so she could spot me when I came out. But she wasn't anywhere!

Maybe she hadn't gotten our last letter and thought I wasn't coming. Or could a person get caught in a traffic jam here? Maybe she'd had an accident on the way from Constantine. That was where she worked, and I had seen on the map that it was quite a distance from Algiers.

I looked around again and noticed a place to change money. I decided to get one of my checks changed to Algerian money. If she hadn't shown up by the time I finished that, then—I wasn't sure what. I didn't know anyone else in this whole country.

The bills they gave me had many colors on them, not just green and black like our dollars. The money was called dinars, and one dinar equaled about twenty-five cents.

I hated to look again, almost sure I would not find Lillian. And I was right. She just wasn't there! I thought of calling the American Embassy. Maybe they could tell me what to do or where to go. But I didn't know how to use the phones here. And wouldn't everyone be talking Arabic or French on them? Should I just wait? Surely there would soon be some message if she didn't arrive.

My thoughts were interrupted by someone calling my name. I looked up just in time to see Lillian dashing toward me. She looked as I'd remembered her—slim, short brown hair with some gray streaks, and a friendly smile. She hugged me, then looked at her watch.

"I'm terribly sorry. I hope you haven't been too worried. I planned to be here early. I do have a good excuse, even though you're probably thinking there couldn't be one. I remember how I felt arriving here the first time, and I was nearly twice your age," she went on.

It seemed as though I didn't have to reply. And I was feeling much better already.

"Oh, I wasn't *too* worried," I fibbed. "Didn't you get our last letter?"

"Oh, yes. Let's go to the car, and then I'll tell you what happened," she said.

She took my suitcase, and I followed with my shoulder bag. She tossed the suitcase in the back seat of her little French car, and we got in front. Putting her hands on the steering wheel, she sighed. "I almost feel like I need to catch my breath, I've been hurrying so."

"What happened?"

"Well, I was nearly ready to leave Constantine to come to meet you when I was called in by the police—the secret police we call them—a bit like the FBI. It's the same office where those of us who aren't tourists, but who work here, get our long-term visas. Sometimes they question us about our work when we go to have our visas renewed.

"Well, my visa hadn't expired," Lillian continued, "so I was surprised to be called in. They asked me all sorts of questions, about who I know and what I've been doing, going way back ten years ago. I'm not sure what the point of it was or why.

"Anyhow, I was free to go after the questioning, but I got started more than an hour later than I'd planned," Lillian said. "I thought I might make it on time. Also I figured it would be better just to keep driving rather than to stop and try to phone someone to meet you."

I didn't understand all this police business. But she didn't seem too worried and had arrived— and that was the most important!

"Now I guess I'm unwound enough to drive you into town," Lillian said. "I thought we could spend a day or two in Algiers, and then we'll head toward Constantine, and see some sights along the way."

Going down the drive leading from the airport, we passed through a double row of palm trees with their high branches arched in spiky curves against the blue sky.

I didn't notice it then, but I wonder now if the black car may have already been following us.

Then we turned left and headed west toward Algiers. When we passed through a small town, I

21

stared at the men in the streets. They wore flowing white robes and turbans which were wound round and round their heads. Other men were dressed in ordinary pants and jackets, but the unusual garb was more interesting to me.

We also went by modern-looking factories. Then our route followed next to the beach, and I could see close at hand the rippling blue-green waves of the Mediterranean Sea.

"Will I get to swim in it sometime?" I asked eagerly.

"It's still early in the season," Lillian said, "but maybe tomorrow we can at least go to the beach."

And then the sea disappeared from view, shut off by the apartment buildings and shops which crowded closely around us as we drove further into the capital city.

No sleep, and the change in time, and the worry of thinking I'd been stranded at the airport made me almost ready to collapse. So not all of Lillian's explanations as we drove through the city registered. But I remember a few groggy impressions— narrow streets, rushing cars and people, women covered with white veils so that only their eyes showed, and the flowing curves and dots of Arabic writing. It was everywhere—on the street signs, on the shop fronts, and in the advertising on the sides of buses.

I was too tired to notice much about where we finally stopped. I just lay down on the bed she piloted me to, blinked once, and was fast asleep.

No dreams disturbed my sleep—because I had no idea then of the things that were waiting to happen.

When I woke up several hours later, I discovered we were in the apartment of some of Lil's friends. (She said she wasn't used to being called "Lillian" and besides, it took too long to say.) These friends were out of town and had said we could stay there.

Lil had slept too, but obviously not as long as I had, because she had sandwiches prepared when I came to.

"Did you see anything the last half of the trip here?" she asked. "You looked like a zombie!"

"Not too much," I had to admit.

"It's four o'clock now," she said. "I thought maybe we could walk around awhile and I can introduce you to the neighborhood."

That sounded good to me, so we finished our sandwiches and were soon on our way. On the first floor of the apartment building were a bakery shop and a tiny grocery store. According to Lil, having stores on the first floor of apartment buildings was not unusual. Much of the bread in the bakery window was French-style—long narrow loaves. But flat round Arabic bread was available also. "There's not so much of that for sale because a lot of people, if they want Arabic bread, bake their own at home," Lil remarked.

I looked around as we strolled up the street. There didn't seem to be a level spot in Algiers. The city was built on the sides of high hills, and everything went up or down. Not far along the street leading away from the apartment building, I almost thought I'd come to the edge of a precipice. I could see the roofs of houses below me. And straight across from us another hill had houses clinging to its steep sides. They seemed close, but to get there would mean a long trip down into the valley and back up the other side.

We soon passed the only open space where we could look down and across, because everywhere there was a spot level enough and wide enough, houses had been built which blocked the view. At least I supposed they were houses. All we could see from the street were walls on both sides. In the walls were doors with numbers beside them. Each numbered door meant a home behind the wall, Lil explained, but we couldn't see them.

"Algerians like their privacy," she said. "Most of these along here are just one or two-room houses, but there could be a mansion and you wouldn't be able to see it either."

We came to a section of stores. "We're staying in the suburb of *El Biar* (The Wells)," she said, "and this is 'downtown' El Biar."

What impressed me was how small the stores were and how each one sold only one thing—I was used to department stores and supermarkets. Here one shop had fresh fruits and vegetables, the next one bread and pastries, another canned foods, the following milk and cheese, then one with shoes, another with meat, followed by one with dishes and gadgets.

When we crossed to the other side of the street, Lil stopped at one of the vegetable shops and got several tomatoes. Then she bought a loaf of bread

at a bakery, and some milk at a dairy shop. The milk came in plastic bags. All of this fit easily into a stretchy plastic net shopping bag she had brought along.

I noticed everyone was carrying their own shopping bags or the limber baskets called *couffins* to hold the things they bought. No wasteful paper bags were used here.

When we arrived back at the apartment, Lil told me to go to the roof and take a look around while she prepared supper. Following her directions, I went out into the hall and up the stairway two more flights. The stairs opened onto the flat roof of the building. From there I could look down on rooftops of other nearby buildings. Some of them were busy places. Laundry was drying on lines, and I could see large containers like basins that women had used to wash the clothes by hand. On other roofs children were playing or mothers were kneading bread. Parts of some rooftops were covered with vegetables spread out to dry—tomatoes and several kinds of peppers.

Up on their roofs, out of sight of the street, the women weren't dressed in veils, but they covered their hair with colorful scarves and wore a kind of baggy trousers (or skirts?). Lil told me they were made with a long piece of material folded in half with the fold at the bottom. The sides were sewed together nearly to the bottom, leaving slits on each side for the legs. Then elastic was sewed all around the top edge to gather it together.

Some of the larger houses had open courtyards in the middle. In these big houses, the courtyards were the scene of the same activities that I had seen on the roofs of the smaller homes.

I went to the other side of our rooftop and stopped, staring in happy surprise. El Biar was on a hilltop, and I could see much of the rest of the city of Algiers dropping away below me, down, down, till it reached the sea.

The daytime blues of sky and sea were fading now, turning to shades of violet and pink. The bottom edges of a few long low purple clouds were outlined in pink-gold. Disappearing behind the horizon, the sun tipped the waves in its path with pink-gold.

After a light supper of soup, tomato salad, bread, and milk, I went with Lil to a Bible study and discussion group. Unfortunately for me, it was all in French. I tried to pick out some words I knew, and did find one or two. But usually the sounds came so fast and were so blended together that I couldn't separate them into words.

When we sang hymns I could follow along, and also when we read from the Bible.

Afterward I met people from France, England, Germany, Norway, and the Netherlands. It seemed strange that they could come from all those different places and learn to understand each other in French, a language which wasn't native to most of them. They nearly all spoke good English, too. When I thought that, like me, most Americans don't know any foreign language, it was embarrassing. Some of these people were teachers, others worked for oil companies, and still others were advisers of one kind or another in factories or businesses that their governments had in Algeria.

On our drive back to the apartment, I asked Lil about one thing I had noticed. "It was interesting to meet people from so many places, but why weren't there any Algerians there?"

"I'm sure you know from what your parents have told you that nearly all Algerians are Muslims."

"Yes, but there are *some* Algerian Christians, aren't there? And isn't that why you're here—to be a missionary and to help Algerians to become Christians?"

"To your first question, yes there are some Algerian Christians, but mighty few compared to the total number of Algerians—perhaps a hundred or so out of thirteen million people. It seems we can best help the Algerian Christians by staying away from them. I know that sounds awful—like segregation or something. It's hard for Algerians to be Christians in the first place. If they associate with foreigners, it's even more difficult for them."

"But why?"

"People here think of Christianity as a foreign religion which has nothing to do with Algerian life. If someone is interested in such a religion and is friends with foreigners, he is under suspicion—it's thought he might be disloyal to his country.

"As for my reason for being here—I could just as well be teaching English in a high school or college in the United States or Canada. So it's not the job in itself. And I do call myself a teacher rather than a missionary. Otherwise I wouldn't even be in this country."

"What do you mean?"

"They don't want anyone in their country whose only job is to take people away from their religion. But I think people in Muslim countries should have a chance to know some real live Christians. Their only ideas of Christianity come from the Crusades, you know, back in the Middle Ages when so-called Christians came here to fight, and kill, and conquer the Muslims."

Now she was starting to sound like a teacher giving a lecture. But I wanted to know more, so I kept listening.

"More recently, the French, who came here as conquering settlers, represented Christianity to them. And many of these French felt superior to the Algerians. They called the Algerians *ratons* (little rats). Many French 'Christians' drank wine, which is against Muslim belief. And many refused to let Algeria become independent from France, so there was a long bloody war between them. Such people are 'Christians' to the Algerians."

"I don't get it. There's no way those things are Christian."

"Europe, America, and Canada are called 'Christian lands.' So to most Algerians 'Christian' means someone from those countries. We make the same mistake if we consider all Algerians Muslim, although many of them might not practice their religion."

"I see what you're getting at," I said.

"If at least some Algerians can realize what a real Christian is, then something will have been accomplished," Lil continued. "But if some Algerians also want to know more about the Jesus of the

Christians and grow to love and follow Him—well that's my fondest hope and dream. And it happens sometimes."

"Why did you say 'the Jesus of the Christians'?"

"Because Jesus is also in the Koran, the Muslims' holy book. But there He's just a prophet, not God's Son. As I mentioned before, it's hard for an Algerian to be a Christian. It can mean losing family and friends and a job. It may mean losing the chance of finding someone to marry, because marriages are usually arranged by the person's family. Christians need the church to be their family, but there are not enough of them. And we Christians from other lands, who'd like to support them, can do more harm than good if we're too friendly."

It gave me a strange feeling. I hadn't yet made a decision to be a Christian. But I assumed I would—I had been brought up to love God and Jesus. And I knew that when I took this step, it would be a happy time for my family and for my friends at church. What would it be like to know that to follow Jesus would mean losing my family and friends? I wanted people to like me, to think well of me, to laugh with me. I didn't know if I'd want to become a Christian either, if I had been born into a Muslim family in Algeria.

The next day was for sight-seeing. First we drove through the part of El Biar where we'd shopped the evening before, and then along a curving road. Through some of the iron-grilled gates we passed we could catch glimpses of luxurious villas surrounded by gardens of palms and flowers. Some of them were embassies of foreign countries. We could tell this by the guards in front, the emblems beside the gates, and the flags flying inside.

Lil drove slowly past one of the gates. "This is *La Palmeraie* (The Palm Grove or The Oasis), a Methodist church center," she said. "It's a beautiful place for all Christians to gather. And there's a library and study center where people coming to Algeria can study Arabic and take courses to learn about North African culture and history. A meeting for young people starts here tonight and runs through tomorrow. I think they'll be mostly older high school and university students. They're a little older than you, but it would be a chance for you to see what the young people here are like. If you're interested, I can check with Ruth and see if you could take in the first part of it."

I thought I probably wouldn't get too much out of it, with the differences in language and age, but still I wanted to use every opportunity I could to learn about Algeria.

"I'd like at least to see what it's like," I said. "But how does a gathering like this fit in with what you were saying about us keeping away from Algerian Christians?"

"It's true that the church is sponsoring this meeting, but it's not a religious get-together. Most of the young people who are coming probably aren't Christians. This is just a chance for young people to get together and get acquainted and discuss things."

"I see," I said. "That should give me a chance, then, to see what some of the Algerian young people are really like and to learn something about their interests."

The Palmeraie was soon forgotten in the excitement of sight-seeing. What I saw first were a *mithrab,* a *minbar,* and a *minaret.* If I tell you that these were all part of a mosque, does that help? Or maybe some of you don't know what a mosque is either. But you like to learn new things (at least *once* in awhile), right?

Well, a mosque is the nearest Muslim thing to our church buildings. By now I've seen them in many shapes and sizes, but they all have the three

M's—minaret, minbar, and mithrab. The minaret is the first thing you notice on a mosque—it's the tall steeple-like tower at one corner of the building. Near the top, a little balcony goes all the way around it. This is where the mosque leader goes to call out over the town or city that it's time for prayer. He says in Arabic, "There is no god but God, and Muhammad is his apostle. Come to prayer. Come to good. Prayer is better than sleep."

Sometimes nowadays the balcony is no longer used for a man to give the call to prayer. Instead, a loudspeaker booms out a recorded call to prayer. Either way, recorded or in person, this chant echoes from the minaret five times a day.

We were near a mosque when I first heard that haunting cry. I expected to see everyone drop what they were doing and to go to the mosque or to kneel right where they were. But hardly anyone seemed to notice it was prayer time. Only a few old men entered the mosque doors. And one wrinkled, be-turbaned fellow rolled out a small rug in front of his shop. There, paying no attention to the people walking by on the busy street, he knelt, rose, knelt, stretched out, rose, and knelt again, all the time chanting his prayer in Arabic.

When the prayer time was over, we went to the mosque, first taking off our shoes and leaving them by the door. I was curious to see the inside of it.

"There certainly weren't many people here praying," I said as we entered.

"You'd see more on Friday," Lil commented. "That's their holy day. But how about your church back home? How many come to prayer meeting? Or maybe there isn't even such a thing anymore."

That was true enough, I thought. People seem to be pretty much the same, no matter where they live or what their religion is.

"This mosque is unusual in the way it's built," she said as we were looking around. "It was a Catholic cathedral, and when Algeria became independent from France in 1962, the new government immediately changed it into a mosque."

I couldn't understand why she was half-smiling as she said it.

"I don't really think that was very nice," I stated.

"Well, in this case I wouldn't complain, because there was a mosque here first of all, and the French replaced it with the cathedral. So now they're even."

The inside of the mosque was simple, yet fancy. It was simple because there were no benches or chairs, only mats and rugs on the floor for kneeling to pray. And there were no pictures of any kind. The fanciness came from the walls decorated with verses from the Koran, written in Arabic in colorful, swirling designs.

Lil saw me looking and said, "It's pretty, isn't it? Islam forbids any kind of pictures, even of animals or nature, to avoid bringing to mind anything but God. Because of this they decorate their buildings with writing or with geometric designs."

As for the mithrab, it was a little niche in one wall showing the direction of Mecca. When worshipers face the mithrab, they know they are praying toward their holy city of Mecca in Arabia. The minbar was a kind of fancy pulpit from which the *imam* (holy man) could speak to the people.

I wished I could have seen the prayers in progress, but prayer is not exactly a spectator sport, and neither women or non-Muslims (and we were both) would be welcome at prayer time.

Near the mosque we went into the government tourist office, formerly the home of the Catholic archbishop. In the center of the building was a courtyard with a fountain in the middle. Archways supported by spiraled columns surrounded the courtyard. They were decorated with tiles in beautiful colors and designs. Back under the arches and pillars was a walk or porch, and from that, doors opened into the various rooms. On the second story the porch became a balcony with a fancy carved-wood railing. I liked this house. It was built in the style the Turks brought when they once ruled North Africa.

From there it was not far to the Casbah, the oldest part of the city. Its narrow streets seemed more like sidewalks. No vehicles could travel them because they were so narrow and steep. In some especially steep places the streets became stairways. Often the buildings' upper stories almost touched each other above our heads, creating a dark tunnel to walk through.

Many of the little shops there were not much different from those we'd seen in El Biar, but the dark streets, twisting and narrow, made everything seem more mysterious. But there were also some more unusual shops. In one the *clank, clank* of workmen hammering designs onto huge copper and brass trays greeted our ears. Other craftsmen were piecing leather into turned-up pointy-toed slippers and footstools and handbags. Some were stitching up hand-woven woolen material into wrap-around burnooses or fashioning the hooded coats called *kashabias*.

We didn't really explore far into the Casbah—it was too much like walking into a maze. "They say you won't get lost if you remember to head downhill—you'll eventually come out at the bottom edge of the Casbah, near the sea," Lil said. "Shall we go on farther?"

I wasn't feeling so adventurous as to want to wander very far from the light and openness of the rest of the city, especially when I noticed a man who seemed to keep watching us. I mentioned this to Lil and pointed him out. He was not very noticeable—dark hair like everyone else, light blue shirt, and dark blue trousers. He might have been following us for sometime without my having seen him.

When she looked, of course he wasn't paying any attention to us, but was talking to a fruit merchant nearby. Lil looked at me and laughed.

"He *was* watching us," I said.

"No doubt. Watching women is a favorite pastime in Algeria—and most everywhere else, for that matter. But especially here, where many women aren't allowed to go out, or if they do, they always veil themselves. So anyone unveiled can almost be sure of being stared at. And then we're

The dark streets, twisting and narrow, made everything seem mysterious in the Casbah section of the city.

foreigners too, so that maybe rates an extra stare."

Well, I wasn't convinced. I thought I was probably too young for much staring and that Lil was too old (but I didn't want to tell her that!).

"Let's go back," I said, so we turned around and headed toward where we'd left our car and entered the Casbah. When we'd gone about halfway down the street, I stopped to glance back. It was dark, but I thought I saw that same blue-shirted figure following us, weaving his way among the people in the street behind us.

At noon we bought some bread and cheese and oranges and drove west along the sea until we were out of the city. Lil was right. It was still too early in the year to think of swimming. The water was cold. But the sun was bright, and its golden touch felt warm on my pale winter skin. The white sand sparkled and poured its warm grains between my toes and over my bare feet as I walked through it.

The beach wasn't too crowded (certainly no blue-shirted man, I noted), so we easily found a spot to eat our picnic. We went as close to the water as we could and still have dry sand to sit on. It was relaxing to sit and watch the waves advance, fold themselves over, and slide back in never-ending rhythm and to listen to their constant *splash-swish, splash-swish*.

"Would you like to go to a museum yet?" Lil asked after we'd finished eating and had been stretched out on the sand awhile. "We should start for Constantine tomorrow morning rather early, after I pick you up at the Palmeraie, so anything else you want to see in *Alger* (she used the French name for Algiers, pronounced al-zhay), we should do this afternoon."

"Sounds good to me," I said. Sometimes I like museums and sometimes I don't, depending on what's in them. I was glad this time that I'd said yes. The museum, called *Musée Bardo*, was in a beautiful old villa. Again there were columns and arches and beautiful tiles and fountains like we'd seen in the archbishop's home-tourist office, plus trees and flowers in some of the courtyards.

I liked the displays of costumes and crafts, many arranged in different rooms to show how people lived in different regions of Algeria—in the desert, in the city, in the different tribes. Besides that, there were rock paintings from the Sahara Desert. According to these ancient pictures, at one time it hadn't been a desert at all, but the home of many animals and people.

Some of the displays I didn't look at much. They contained some crude tools which showed that people were living in North Africa way back in pre-historic stone-age times.

Then we went back to the apartment for something to eat, and Lil phoned her friend Ruth to see if it would be okay for me to participate in the youth meeting that evening and to stay overnight there. It was.

All I took along was my toilet kit and pj's. Lil would bring my suitcase when she picked me up in the morning to start our drive to Constantine.

"I wouldn't mind being in on this meeting, too, since I teach university students at Constantine," she remarked as we pulled up at the Palmeraie.

"Well, why aren't you?" I asked.

"They want to keep the foreigners at a minimum. It's for the Algerian people, not for our benefit."

"Then I shouldn't be here. Or you should take my place."

"No, that's okay. I should have said 'keep the foreign *adults* at a minimum.' I don't think you'll put a damper on things, but I would be an extra person they don't need."

Lil was more right than she knew, not to stay.

She left me with Ruth, a Swiss missionary, who took me upstairs in one of the buildings and showed me where the other girls and I would sleep. I left my things on a cot there and went with her to the building next door, where everyone was gathering. There she introduced me to a few young people, and then left to take care of other new arrivals.

I'm rather shy, and knowing that I didn't really belong, didn't help—not to mention not being able to say much more than "Bonjour." So I just sat quietly and watched. Everyone seemed in good spirits, ready to enjoy this weekend together during their spring break. They looked much like the youth group from my home church, except perhaps not as many of the girls here wore jeans, and more of the kids had black hair and darker skin.

The meeting began with a speaker addressing the group. That's when I noticed how tired I was. I suppose it was partly from not being able to understand what was going on and partly from the full day we'd had. And probably I wasn't yet completely recovered from the night of sleep I'd lost on my flight over. So to keep awake I counted the people there—forty altogether, including the six non-Algerian Methodists who had organized the weekend.

But the counting didn't take long, and I was getting drowsy again. Then the speaker stopped, and they began a question-and-answer and discussion period. Since I could understand even less of that, it didn't help my sleepiness.

But when some guitars came on the scene, and a time of singing began, my interest perked up. When I heard a familiar tune, I tried to see if the words they were singing were a translation of the English ones, or if they had other words to the same tune.

I was just too weary, though, and the singers sounded like they could keep going for hours. So in spite of my wanting to be where the "action" was, I gave up.

The singing followed me as I stepped outside, walked to the other building and up the stairs. I could still hear the sounds of music and laughter as I put on my pajamas and drifted off to sleep.

I blinked my eyes open. It was still early—light enough to see, but the light was grayish rather than the bright yellow of full sunlight. I could hear birds twittering in the garden.

I remembered where I was then, and sat up carefully so that I wouldn't wake the other girls. Maybe they had gone to bed quite late. I didn't know for sure because I hadn't heard them come in.

As I began to take off my pajamas, I looked around in surprise. The others—they weren't there! No one was in the other beds. How strange that they would be up and around this early, and that I hadn't heard them get up. I put on my glasses so I could see better. Then I looked again. I walked slowly around the room. None of the beds had been slept in!

Had they kept up their singing and talking all night? But it seemed unnaturally quiet. There was no sound at all except for the birds. Perhaps they'd fallen asleep in the meeting room? That must be it.

I finished dressing hurriedly, ran a comb through my short dark hair, and dashed downstairs. I hesitated, almost afraid to look in the meeting room. But I made myself go in. It was empty. Guitars were lying there as if they'd been suddenly dropped, and a few soft drink bottles were scattered around.

"Is . . . is anyone here?" I called faintly. There was no one . . . anywhere.

Could they be out walking in the gardens? Somehow I knew they weren't—but how could forty people simply vanish? It was as if one moment they'd been there, singing and playing—and the next, they were gone.

Yet I went out to look. Back along the path was another building. Lil had said it was the chapel with classrooms and an apartment and the study center. I knocked. Nothing. I opened the door and went in. I called out. No answer.

I opened another door. It was the church office. A phone. I'd call Lil. Then I realized I didn't know where to call. Lil was not in her own apartment, and I didn't know whose it was.

I began to feel panicky. What could I do? I grabbed the phone book and found "Methodist." Under it I found La Palmeraie and the number where I was. But there were other numbers too. Should I try one of those? I had to do something.

I dialed one of them. After six rings, a man's voice answered, "Allo?"

"Do you speak English?"

"Yes."

"I'm at the Palmeraie, for the youth meeting. I got up this morning, and there's no one here. They've all disappeared!"

"What? Who are you?"

I told him who I was and then went through the story of how I'd gone to bed early and what I'd found or hadn't found this morning.

He told me he was William Ward, that he would be there in about fifteen minutes, and that I should be at the gate to meet him. Also he knew Lil and thought his wife would know where she was staying and would have her call Lil before he left.

I felt relieved to have talked to another person— at least I was not the only one left in the world. I went back and got my overnight kit and pajamas and walked through the gardens toward the road. Then I saw that there were still other people around besides Mr. Ward and me. Two men in uniform were standing guard at the gate. I stopped. What were they doing there? What would they do if they saw me?

A car pulled up as if to drive in but was stopped by the police. A man got out and began talking to them. The expression on his face became shocked, unbelieving. He spoke to them some more, then they all turned and looked toward me.

"Is that you, Zina?" he called. It was Mr. Ward. I recognized his voice and hurried to the gate. He talked to the police some more and they shook their heads. I was sure they were talking about me.

About then Lil drove up, got out of her car, and joined in the conversation.

"Oh, no," she said. "Oh, no."

Then I think they talked some more about me. All at once one of the policemen turned to me and fired a question. I just stared at him stupidly. He barked the question again.

"*Je ne sais pas,*" I said slowly. "I mean, *je ne comprends pas.*" (I had meant to say, "I don't understand," but had by mistake first said, "I don't know.")

He shrugged his shoulders and gave me a push toward Lil. She took my hand, and with her other hand shook hands with Mr. Ward and kissed him on the cheek, saying, "Goodbye, Bill. And thanks. I'll call Jane and tell her what's happened." And we went to her car.

I looked back as we drove off and saw that a police car had arrived and that Mr. Ward was being put into it. I still had no idea of what was happening.

"Lil, tell me!"

"Just be thankful you didn't understand what they said to you, or you'd be going with Bill to the police station. He tried to convince them you didn't know anything about what had happened, and you helped him do it."

"Well, that wasn't hard to do, because I don't."

"I can't believe it. The police told him everyone

was taken off to jail last night."

"But there were forty people!"

"Everyone. They didn't realize that you were upstairs sleeping. The six other foreigners who were there have already left the country. They've been expelled. And all the Algerians are still at police headquarters, being questioned."

"But why? They were only singing and talking."

"I don't know. I can't imagine. We'll go pick up our suitcases and then head east. I think the sooner we leave Algiers, the better."

We quickly got our suitcases ready, and Lil called Bill's wife. I heard her tell her what had happened and add at the end, "They took him along to police headquarters, Jane. I'm so afraid that—you mustn't be surprised if he gets thrown out like the others."

When we left the apartment, Lil bought a morning paper from the newsstand on the sidewalk. She quickly glanced through it before starting up the car.

"It's in the paper already. They were expelled 'for subversive activities,' it says. Ha! It also says the army will be taking over the property. That's probably part of the reason this happened. That's a really nice piece of land and fine buildings at a very desirable location—all gone to the government for free."

I still couldn't take everything in. All those kids, so full of life and fun, were in jail now. And Ruth and the others were gone, taking nothing with them, probably never to return. Only I was left. It really wouldn't have mattered as much if it had happened to me as to them. I would have been unhappy and scared, but I wouldn't have lost everything.

Snow-capped mountains! I hadn't expected to see that in Algeria. But there they were, majestic faraway peaks rising to the north of us.

We had left Algiers about eight o'clock that morning, going east by the same route we'd taken into the city when I'd arrived by plane.

The scenery took my mind off what had happened the night before—at least part of the time. We had passed through an area of vineyards on the flat plains around Algiers. These grapevines had been planted by the French to use for producing wine. Now the French are gone, and Muslims are not supposed to drink alcohol, so most of the wine is shipped to other countries. In some places, vineyards have been torn out and grain planted instead.

Beyond the plains we had come into a region of pale green hills. It was the young barley and wheat covering them which made them that color. Some of them were splotched with darker green where clumps of olive trees grew. And then *Lalla Khedidja* (Mrs. Khedidja, as one of the mountains was named) loomed into view behind the hills, she and her other snow-topped friends.

"I wish we had time to drive back through the mountains," Lil said, "so you could see a Kabyle village. Each one is perched on its own mountaintop, like a fortress-town from ancient times. The Kabyles are one of Algeria's Berber tribes."

That didn't tell me much until she explained that the Berbers were the first people to live in North Africa. No one knows for sure where they came from—perhaps Europe. They lived here before any of the long list of invaders and conquerors who came one after the other—first the Phoenicians, then Romans, Vandals, Arabs, Turks. And last, the French. Through all this, the Kabyles kept their own language and customs, although they adopted the Islamic religion from the Arabs.

When she mentioned the names of Kabyle towns like Benni Yenni and Tizi-Ouzou and told of the colorful dress of the women, when she described the beautiful baskets and blankets they wove, I wanted to leave the modern highway we were speeding along and see for myself the life in one of these villages.

But I had to be content with wondering what it would be like. There wasn't time. "Besides," Lil said when she saw my longing glances toward the mountains, "You're supposed to visit your parents' friends later on. They're *Chaouias*, and that's another Berber group. You'll see village life when you visit them."

As the road veered south a little, the mountains faded in the distance. We were entering a region of immense slightly rolling plains—the high plateaus. There were few trees, just the green-wheat-covered hills. Some places a few wild flowers dotted the green with violet, yellow, and white.

"This place looks quite different at various times of the year," Lil said. "Soon the wild flowers will be out in full force. They're just gorgeous then, covering entire fields. But after the harvest everything will be brown and dry and dead-looking until the green shoots of wheat appear the next spring."

This scenery should have been boring, but somehow the quiet and peace of its stretching sameness had its own kind of beauty.

We arrived at Setif, not so large a town, but the largest one since Algiers. Our trip was about two thirds over now. After five hours of traveling, we were famished, tired of driving, and glad to stop and buy some bread and cheese and fruit. The cheese this time was little foil-wrapped triangles, the bread was long skinny extra-crisp baguettes, and the fruit was grapes.

"That car stopped at Setif, too," I said when we were returning to our car with our purchases.

"What car?"

"Oh, that black one over there that's been following us ever since Algiers."

"Well, this is the only main route to Constantine," she said, dismissing my worry, "so anyone going there has to travel this road."

But I was uneasy, especially after last night's experience. Still, they had let me go.

We were quickly on our way again, both eager for the detour coming up. We planned to go thirty kilometers north of the main road to see Djemila. Djemila is a girl's name meaning "beautiful," but in this case, it's also the name of a town—a ghost town. Unlike the 100-year-old gold-rush ghost towns of the Western United States, this town is nearly two thousand years old.

As our road curved among the hills, I looked back and thought I saw that same black car. So they were going to visit Djemila too? Then just as it seemed we were far from any trace of civilization, the next curve revealed Djemila, a city of stone. Built by the Romans, much of it was still standing for us to see—columns, arches, walls—their ancient stones glowing golden in the sun.

Walking into this old city was like taking a giant step back in time. Some of the stone streets had grooves for the chariot wheels to roll in. I almost expected to see Ben Hur flash around one of the corners. We went into houses with enough walls and doorways still standing so you could walk from one room to the other, from one building to another. But overhead there were no ceilings, only the blue sky.

"We'll stop at the museum beside the ruins later," Lil said. "There they have, for safe-keeping, the mosaic designs which the Romans used to

The Roman temple honoring Jupiter was partly destroyed, but many of the columns which flanked its sides were still standing.

50

decorate the floors of their homes. And they have some statues too."

From the houses we went to the theater, a huge semicircle of stone seats, rising steeply row after row. Had the people of Cuicul, as Djemila was then called, come to watch plays here? Or did they perhaps come to listen to some great speaker?

Other stones formed a great arch for the army to march through, and still others had been used to build a temple. It was partly destroyed, but you could still climb the steps to the entrance, and many of the columns which flanked it on both sides were still standing.

"Is this temple for one of the Roman gods?" I asked.

"Yes. It was built to honor Jupiter, the king of the gods. There's a building further on which was a Christian place for baptism."

"Huh? Used by whom?"

"By the Christians who lived here. In the early days after Christ, North Africa was Christian. The Book of Acts says that one of the people who brought the news of Jesus to Antioch was from Cyrene, and so was the man who helped Jesus carry His cross. Cyrene is today the city of Kairouan in Tunisia. And one of the great early Christians, St. Augustine, lived in Annaba, an Algerian city which the Romans called Hippo."

It was hard to imagine that this whole area had once had many Christians.

"What happened?" I asked.

"All kinds of disputes about beliefs and practices divided the Christians. By the time Islam was spreading in the 600s, the church had become weak and unattractive. Christianity faded and Islam took over."

Jupiter's temple was in ruins. But so were the Christian buildings of Djemila. But there wasn't time then to think about what this meant. We were continuing our tour and looking at relics of the everyday life of the people.

We saw toilets carved out of stone and, in the marketplace, a stone table where merchants measured their grain. Funnel shapes of three sizes were carved in the table. One of these would be filled with grain. Then the buyer would place his sack underneath, a stopper was removed, and the measured grain flowed into the sack below.

Lil said, "When I see how the Romans lived, I begin to wonder how much progress we've actually made in the two thousand years since then. They had many practical ways of doing things—all without using electricity, gas, oil, or coal."

"Yeah," I said. "In the United States we have a fuel crisis of some kind every year. But I don't see how we could get along without cars and electricity and all the things we're used to. I can't imagine how people lived then."

Lil laughed. "It's not only back then that people didn't have electric appliances and cars. When we visit your parents' friends, you'll see that plenty of people live like that now too."

I didn't see the black car in the parking lot as we went to leave. But when we got to the town where we once more returned to the main route, we passed a parked car which looked the same. This time I saw the driver. Was it a trick of my imagination, or was he the same man I had seen in the Casbah? When the car started up soon after we'd passed it and headed the same direction as we were going, I was almost sure that I hadn't been mistaken. But I didn't say anything to Lil.

The kilometers rolled on. We were still in the empty endless plateau country. Sometimes the thin soil had been washed and blown away, leaving rocky hills and mountains standing above the plains. Their gray sides made the landscape seem strange and hostile.

It was dark by the time we neared Constantine. The closer we came to the city, the more the traffic increased, making it impossible to tell if among the many headlights behind us were those of the black car.

The evening before it had been too dark to see much of anything, so it was not until the next day that I really saw Constantine. And what I saw then when we traveled around astonished me.

I was impressed by the contrasts of the old and the new, the rich and the poor, everywhere. For instance, the people's homes. Immense sleek high-rise apartment buildings towered above *gourbis* (shacks made of scrap materials), and peaky, striped-wool nomad tents squatted in their shadows. Villas with gardens of flowers contrasted sharply with the Constantine version of the Algiers Casbah—a narrow, dark, going-in-all directions maze of streets.

In the "downtown" shopping area the contrasts continued. There were large department-type stores and mini-shops, automobiles and donkeys. Businessmen in suits and ties and villagers with turbans and kashabias mingled in the same streets.

But most astonishing was the way the city was built and where it was built. I found that out after we crossed a suspension bridge swaying over a gorge below, too far below for me to want to look. From the bridge we went up a sharply winding road which ended near a huge arch.

"It's called the 'Monument to the Dead,'" Lil said. "The names of the Algerian and French who died in World War I are engraved inside. You may not be interested in this, but I like to come because of the wonderful view from up here."

The stone steps we were going up brought us nearer the massive structure. A statue with flowing robes and outstretched wings was perched on top of it. It might represent France or victory. I wasn't sure, and Lil didn't know either. On each side of the arch were empty niches where statues of French generals had once stood. These had silently disappeared when Algeria became independent from France in 1962.

We walked under the arch. At the other side and circling nearly around the arch was a platform. At the edge we could look down and see the city spread out below.

The old part of the city is built on a high, thrusting plateau surrounded on three sides by steep rocky gorges. But by now the city has spread itself out much further in all directions, and a number of bridges span the gorges to connect the old and the new.

"It's a natural place for a fortified city," Lil said. "The gorges made a hard defense for invaders to break through. Even in more modern days when the French came, they had a hard time taking the city. Constantine is old, really old. In the long-ago time before the Romans, it was known as Cirta. Later the Romans named it after their emperor, Constantine. When the Algerians became independent from France, they changed many of the names of the cities and gave them Arabic names. But Constantine kept its name."

Beyond the city, the green rolling plains of the high plateau stretched to the horizon in all directions. Lil pointed south, the direction we would be traveling the next day.

When we drove down from the arch and neared the suspension bridge, we went on by it, past the big Constantine hospital, and then came to a small "maternity clinic"—the place where I was born. We stopped and went inside. I looked around. There were three rooms with four beds in each, mostly empty for the moment, plus a labor and delivery room, and an office for the midwife who ran the clinic.

We talked, or rather Lil did, to the midwife and discovered that she had been there for fifteen years. So maybe she was the very one who delivered me.

"Oh, there have been so many babies, I don't remember," she said when Lil explained who I was.

Then I pulled out the snapshot my parents had given me to bring along, since they'd hoped that I'd be able to see this place where I had made my entry into the world. The picture was taken by my father and showed one of the scratched-up metal beds. On the bed was a smiling young woman proudly holding a neither-cute-nor-ugly little bundle. Beside the bed was the midwife as she had looked fourteen years ago, dressed in a stained white smock which looked like it might be the same one she was wearing now.

She looked closely at the picture. "Yes, I remember now. That was the one where the papa was insisting to be there for the baby's birth. I was insisting no—it is not our way here. And suddenly the baby was coming and I was so busy I could not chase him out. So he was here anyway."

I had heard the story too, although Dad did not tell it in quite the same way. In his version it was their first baby, they were far from home, and they felt the medical attention was not the best. Dad had not been able to have a COA doctor friend be present as he wished, and he was not about to leave Mother alone with "that old dragon," as he referred to the midwife.

At any rate, all had turned out well. At least I never heard them regretting the fact that I had been part of the family from then on.

We thanked the midwife for her time, and went back to the car. Lil drove out of the city now, toward the hills where the University of Constantine is located. This was where she taught English.

The buildings were modern and in a nice setting—away from the city's noise, yet not too far away. In fact, from the campus there was a good view of Constantine.

Most of the students were gone because of spring

break, and the few I did see reminded me too much of the young people I'd seen the night before last.

Lil showed me the room where she did most of her teaching and picked up a book she'd left there. Coming out we met a girl she knew, evidently one of her students, because Lil spoke to her in English.

"Malika, this is Zina. She's visiting me from the United States. I'll be driving through Ain M'Lila tomorrow, taking Zina to visit some of her parents' friends near there. Since you're from Ain M'Lila, maybe you'd want to ride along and visit your family."

"Yes, I think I need to get away. I can finish the paper I'm working on later. And I really should go. I haven't been home for two months now," Malika replied.

We left the university and drove into Constantine, through the old part of the city, and back to Lil's apartment. From there we set out on foot to do more exploring.

One street I was interested in was lined with souvenir shops, selling mostly handcrafted items. I didn't know what to get Mother and Dad at first. They had so many nice things from Algeria already that they had brought back with them. I decided on a book with up-to-date colored photographs from the Constantine area. For myself I got a little engraved copper tray, a leather billfold with a camel embossed on it, and an embroidered jacket.

Then it was time to get back and prepare for some guests Lil was having for supper.

I guess I haven't told you yet about her apartment. I won't describe the usual things, just pick

59

out a few items which were new and different to me. I suppose I could say they are typical, since I saw the same things in other places during my stay in Algeria.

The thing I remember best is the water heater, because it scared me so the first time I turned on the hot water faucet and heard a gigantic "whoosh." This small water heater, run by gas, is located just above the faucets. It heats only when the water is turned on. Then the pilot light connects and the flames whoosh on to warm the water as it flows out. When you close the hot-water faucet, only the pilot light remains lit.

Another energy-saver is the hall lights in the apartment building. When you enter the building, the halls are dark. Push a button and the lights go on, but they automatically go off after thirty seconds, just enough time to light you to the next button on the floor above. On each floor is another button to push if you are going on to the floor beyond.

Electric sockets have round holes, so, of course, the little metal prongs on the plugs are round rather than flat like ours.

The gas stove, water heater, and room heater are run by gas from bottles—the big heavy metal containers the gas comes in. These are connected by rubber tubes to the appliances. You must always have an extra bottle or two on hand so as not to run out while cooking a meal or taking a shower.

The windows don't have shades but shutters which unfolded and really shut. For the first time I realized where shutters got their name, and that they were not meant to be decorations tacked onto a house, but to be used.

Lil had no closets, but big cupboard-like wardrobes to hang clothes in and to store things.

Her telephone bill is determined by how many calls she makes a month, not by a fixed rate. The television set is mostly off. "There's only one channel and usually not much worth watching—which isn't too different from the States, actually," she explained. "There you have four or more channels and still not much worth watching."

I didn't quite agree. But I was surprised that I hadn't missed TV after several days without it. I guess there was too much else more interesting going on. But I did want to see what Algerian TV looked like, so I flicked her set on while we were waiting for the guests to arrive. I soon pushed the off button. *Gunsmoke* in French and the news in Arabic are not my idea of entertainment!

There were three guests for supper that evening—all COA workers. When my parents lived in Algeria a number of COAers had worked as teachers, doctors, nurses, agriculture technicians, and the like. Now there were only these three who had come for two or three years to teach in Algerian high schools. The couple, Bob and Betty Dennis, taught in Laghovat on the edge of the desert, and Carl Morris taught somewhere even further south. They had come north during their spring break to be together and to visit the Constantine area.

It seemed that the short-termers looked on Lil as an adviser. She had been in Algeria a long time and could give them some counsel in their problems. She could help them begin to understand people who had strange customs and a culture quite different from their own.

Through listening to them as they talked, I learned a little about the Algerian school system. It is still much the same as the French had set it up, and that makes it quite different from what I'm used to. For one thing boys and girls usually go to separate schools until they are out of high school and into university. Another difference is the grading system. It's by numbers, usually on a base of 10. That is, 9/10 is a very good grade and 2/10 is a poor one.

And exams are very important. Passing an exam at the end of high school is what gets you your diploma. Failing the exam makes it impossible for you to enter university.

The COAers all taught English as a foreign language. "It's discouraging," Betty Dennis said. "The kids don't work hard at English. They don't think it's important—just because it doesn't count for nearly as many points on the exam as math or science."

"Right," agreed the others. "They just don't care."

"And the discipline!" Bob Dennis said. My ears were wide open. Somehow I'd never thought about teachers talking about the kids and criticizing us the way we do the teachers. I wonder what mine back in South Bend say about me?

"But have you ever seen a high school where discipline's easy?" Carl was asking.

"It's so hard to control cheating on homework," Betty said. It seemed this was because many students were boarding students (they lived at the school), and it was so easy for them to do their homework together.

The teachers had other gripes too. Yet no one seemed really unhappy. "I'm glad we came, in spite of any difficulties," Bob concluded. "We're learning to know new people and another way of living. It feels good to help in the education program of a new nation."

But then the conversation turned to what everyone was concerned and curious about—what had happened in Algiers. What might this expelling of missionaries mean to the rest of them? Lil reported that she had phoned Jane Ward about five o'clock and had found out that Bill had been expelled, too. And Jane had told her that other people, not only from their mission, but also from other church groups and service agencies, were being called in for questioning. The Algerian young people who had been taken in had now been released. But they had been warned to be loyal to their own country and to stay away from the kind of people they'd been found with.

No one knew why this was happening or what it could lead to. They tried to make light of the situation by teasing me. "How could you possibly sleep through something as exciting as that?" Carl asked.

"It was plenty exciting enough to get up and find everyone had vanished," I said, and felt again that strange, unreal sensation I'd felt then.

"Is it true you were called in for questioning,

Lil?" Betty asked. "And do you think it had any connection with this?"

"I was called in. I haven't figured out why yet, but it doesn't seem to be anything to be worried about. I'm still around. And I don't think it has any connection with what happened in Algiers."

"Are you sure?" Carl asked teasingly. "I saw a secret-police type lurking around when we came this evening."

"You're as bad as Zina," Lil said. "She kept thinking we were being followed in Algiers and on our way here."

"Ho, ho. I'd better make sure the lurker is not still lurking then," he said as he strolled over to the little balcony and opened the full-length shutters which served as a door.

He looked a little surprised when he came back to the table.

"So, what did you see?" Lil asked, "Let me guess. The street, two cars, three bicycles, and. . . ."

"Well, actually, the same guy is still standing around down there."

"I think if anyone were really following anyone, they wouldn't be so obvious about it," Lil said, "and there are a hundred other people he could be watching in this building, if he *is* watching anyone. Probably you, Carl. They've heard how the girls in Ghardaia go for you!"

"No doubt. Except that he was here *before* I got here, so it's not me he's after. Well, just beware of a dark man in dark blue trousers and light blue shirt!"

"Oh, no," I thought. "Could it be the same man?"

The next morning we picked up Malika at the university. She was dressed differently from yesterday. She wore a dress instead of jeans and had her hair tucked under a scarf.

As we were going south from the university, we passed near the Constantine airport. Lil said I would fly to Algiers from this airport when I was heading home, since she wouldn't be driving me back to Algiers.

The countryside was much the same as what we had seen on the high plateau between Algiers and Constantine. The few small towns we went through were all alike. There was the main street (our route). In the center of town, main street was always bordered by small stores—a butcher shop, a hardware store, a fabric shop, a café, a post office, the mayor's office. Usually a small mosque (new) poked its square white tower against the blue sky.

And a Catholic church (old), a remnant from the French days, stood nearby. It was either falling into ruin or else was being used as a social center or a meeting place for the scouts. Before and after this "downtown," there were homes on both sides of the street, invisible behind their high whitewashed courtyard walls.

Usually in at least one direction we could see mountains. They were not actually very high, but they seemed quite tall because they rose directly out of the flat land. And their color—was it blue or gray or pinkish? All three, it seemed, depending on the way the sun hit them.

Ain M'Lila, when we finally arrived there, was a town like the others, but we got a closer look at it when we left the main street to follow Malika's directions to her house. Now at last I would get to see what was behind one of those walls, for Malika insisted we should go in with her. The wooden outer door opened onto a tiny courtyard, more like a hallway, and from there we went into a small room.

And we entered a different world from Lil's European-type apartment in the city. Rolled-up blankets stacked against one wall meant that this was a bedroom. But we soon found out it was living room and dining room and kitchen as well.

Malika's mother had not known guests were coming. But in spite of our protests, she quickly began to prepare something to eat. While mother and daughter argued about who would run to the store for something more they needed, I whispered to Lil, "We shouldn't eat anything. It looks like they are rather poor."

Lil answered, "Poor or not, Algerians are always very hospitable. They'd feel insulted if we didn't eat something."

Mother won the argument and I watched, fascinated, as she tied a white nylon triangle shaped "mask" over her face, covering all but her eyes. Next she wrapped herself in a black robe or veil which covered her hair and the rest of her body. Not until then was she ready to venture out of the house. This black *haik* or veil is worn only by women in the Constantine area. In all the rest of Algeria, the women's veils are white.

"I wanted to go to the shop," Malika explained to us when her mother had left, "but Mother doesn't want her neighbors and friends to see me on the streets unveiled, and I will not put on a veil. I already changed the way I usually dress to come here. Mother would be ashamed to see me in jeans or with my hair uncovered."

"Do you think you'll ever wear a veil?" Lil asked

"I hope not. But it will depend whom I marry and where I live. If I live in a village, it would be difficult to go without a veil when everyone else wears one. People think you're a wicked woman without one. Or if I have a strict husband who has traditional ideas, I'll have to wear a veil."

"But why would you marry someone like that?" I asked.

"I must do what my family wants. Many times the parents arrange the marriage, and the groom's father must pay a lot of money or animals to the bride's family."

"But that custom is changing, isn't it?" asked Lil.

"In the big cities, yes. But in a village like this, the old customs are still much the same. If I do what I want and don't listen to my family, then they will disown me. So I don't know. They have one boy picked out for me. But I keep saying I must finish my university courses first. Then if I get a job somewhere else, perhaps I can live how I want to."

As she was talking, Malika placed a small round table in front of us. It was about a foot high. We were sitting on the floor. The only chair in the house had been offered to Lil as a place of honor, but she said she preferred the floor. And so the table was just the right height for us.

Mother returned carrying a bottle of dark red liquid. Malika placed four glasses on the table and filled each one about a third full of the thick red syrup. She added water to fill the glasses. Curiously, I took a sip. I liked the sweet taste. Lil explained to me that you could buy various fruit flavors of syrup, sort of a liquid Kool-Aid, rather than one that came in powder form. This particular flavor was called *grenadine* and was made from pomegranates. When I later saw some in the market, they looked like large oranges with red peelings. Inside they are full of seeds, each seed enclosed in a small coating of red pulp. This pulp is used to make the syrup.

With this drink we had delicious cookies. They were fat and crescent-shaped and rolled in powdered sugar. Under the sugar was a sort of pie crust, and inside that, a stuffing of ground almonds and honey.

After much insisting, we persuaded Malika's mother that we really did not want third helpings of grenadine and "gazelle horns" (the name of the cookies).

We arranged to pick Malika up a few hours later on our return toward Constantine, and then left Ain M'Lila and headed toward an even more remote village. I was to try to find my parents' friends there.

On the way I saw some huge black and white birds. They flew gracefully, with their long skinny reddish legs stretched out behind them and their long red beaks pointing forward.

"Whatever are they?" I asked.

"Storks," was Lil's one-word answer.

I saw their nests, then, clustered on rooftops or sometimes on the tops of electric poles. The storks didn't seem to have any voices, but soared silently through space. The only sound that came from them was an occasional *clack-clack* of their beaks while they were on the nests.

Oh, yes—for those of you who may have heard the rumor that storks bring babies—I looked carefully, and can report that this story is not true!

We came to a small village. When we asked the way to our destination, we found we had to go still farther. A mile out from the village we at last found the Maanser family *mechta*, a group of houses plunked down in the middle of some stony fields. Even though there were from 25 to 30 houses, it was not a village—that is, it had no stores and no streets. The people who live in a mechta are all related, all from one family. When the boys marry, their wives come there to live, and so the mechta grows. (I knew all this from my parents.)

This mechta was where I hoped to find Salim and Mebareka Maanser. My father had taught Salim about raising chickens, and my mother had had Mebareka as a helper in her nursing work in a clinic. Later they had married, and since they were both Maansers, we thought they would be living in the Maanser mechta. They and Mother and Dad had written to each other once in awhile the first few years after my parents had left. But since Salim and Mebareka had had only several years of school (which was more than most others their age), they couldn't write very well, so the letter-writing had stopped.

However, my parents had written to them just before my trip, saying that I would try to come to visit them. But since my folks didn't know for sure where their friends were now, I didn't know whether or not the letter had reached them.

Children came running and cried, *"Roumith, roumith"* (meaning Roman, the word used for white or European females), when we drove up to the mechta and stopped. Their cries brought people scurrying from all over. As I got out of the car, I pulled out the old photos my parents had given me to bring along—one with Dad and Salim and the other showing Mother and Mebareka at work. Then two people, still looking much the same as those in the photos, came out of the crowd which was gathering, and made themselves known to us.

Lil had visited here once years ago during the time when my parents had been working with the

COA team in this valley, and all the Maansers were claiming to remember her from then. They'd seen me too, from age five days to one year, and they were sure they knew me also, although I feel I've changed quite a bit since then!

But the acquaintance was enough that we were welcomed by the women with the greetings usually used only for special people. Let me explain the greeting ritual that I went through with Mebareka. First we gave each other five or so kisses on each cheek. Then our clasped hands went back and forth about five times while she kissed my fingers and I kissed hers. We ended by each placing our index finger on our lips. If I hadn't been told about the greetings in advance by my parents, I would have been flabbergasted. As it was, even with the advance warning, I could hardly believe it.

In coming to this Chaouia mechta, we were even further away from life as I knew it. Lil's apartment had had its little differences which I've described to you. Malika's home in Ain M'Lila had been a bigger change.

But here, in spite of pictures I'd seen, I felt completely away from anything familiar.

Words of all kinds were flying around me in mad confusion. Those who'd been to school in the old days or traveled around a bit were talking in strangely accented French to Lil. Others who'd been to school more recently were trying their Arabic on her. Although her French was very good, her Arabic wasn't, she'd told me. Teaching English did not seem to make it so important for her to be able to speak Arabic, although she had studied

71

quite a bit. But besides the Arabic and French, all the conversation and comments among themselves as they looked us over was in Chaouia, a Berber dialect neither of us knew.

I did try out my *la-bess*, an expression which my parents had remembered. They told me it could be an all-purpose greeting, both to ask, "How are you?" (la-bess?), and to reply, "I'm fine!" (la-bess!). The only other words I knew were *e-rah* for "no" and *ih* for "yes," and they didn't seem to fit in right at the moment!

As the greetings and what seemed to me the hundreds of kisses were nearing an end, we were arriving at Salim and Mebareka's house. It looked like all the others—made of brownish-yellow stones gathered from the fields around, and topped with a red-orange tile roof. We went into the courtyard and sat down on a cloth spread out there for us. The one room of their house was too small to hold all the curious relatives. So was the courtyard, for that matter. I don't know how many people crowded in, but many more were gazing in through the open door in the courtyard wall.

The clothing of the women took my eye. The older ones wore many dresses—at least four or five, and they had woolen shawls pinned around their shoulders. Silver bracelets hung on their arms and around their ankles, and large earrings swayed from their ears as they walked. Enveloping their heads were a remarkable number of colored scarves, somehow woven together to form big turbans. Many of them had fancy geometric designs tattooed in blue on their faces and arms. The younger women and girls were more simply dressed, wearing only two or three dresses, topped with perhaps a frayed sweater or worn velvet jacket, and a scarf, tied in back, on their heads.

I could see that, as at Malika's house, some of the women immediately began to prepare refreshments. Mebareka lit the stove and put on water and coffee to boil in a small black cone-shaped iron container. So that you don't imagine a four-burner electric stove, let me explain that the stove was about a foot and a half high and half that wide. At the bottom was a round flat-shaped container of kerosene with a little knob to pump the kerosene up to the burner at the top. The water for the coffee came from a goatskin hanging on the wall and had probably arrived there on a donkey's back from a well a mile away.

There was a little round low table, and on it were cups so small they looked like toys. I discovered later that they were plenty large enough. Although the actual amount of coffee they contained was small, it was so strong and thick that one small cup of it equaled two normal-sized cups of "regular" coffee. It took two lumps of sugar in one of these small cups of coffee to make it possible for me to drink it. This sugar at least partly neutralized the black pepper which Mebareka had added to the coffee as flavoring.

With the coffee we had some "cookies" made from two layers of coarsely ground meal mixed with honey to hold it together. Sandwiched between the layers was a paste of ground dates. This treat was cut into diamond-shaped pieces. I

73

wasn't too fond of these "cookies," but they helped me to be able to drink the coffee.

Because of the language barrier and because we didn't have too much in common, it was hard to find things to talk about. I gave them the little gifts my parents had sent with me. That took some time. But after showing them the recent photos that I'd brought along of my parents and our house, after repeating several times that my parents were in good health, after accepting their sympathy that my parents had only one child (and a girl at that), and after becoming acquainted with their three children, we had nearly run out of things to talk about.

There was one more subject, though. My parents had wanted to know if anything remained of the work they had done those thirteen years before. Was the clinic still there? Were any of the farmers my dad had helped still raising chickens or gardens? I got Lil to try to ask for me.

It seems there was a clinic at the village twice a week, but the "nurse" who ran it did not have much training, and only the very poorest went there.

Most people no longer had the chicken pens Dad had helped them build, but instead they let a few scrawny chickens run and scavenge, as they had done before. Salim thought he knew of two mechtas which had gardens, but the Maanser mechta didn't. It was too far from water to make a garden practical.

It didn't sound like a very encouraging report to take back to my parents. Lil must have seen that I looked a little disappointed. She said, "Sometimes it's hard to see whether anything's really been accomplished. But I think some good was done. People got some ideas about better, healthier ways to live. And more children are going to school than when your parents were here."

I thought also of the very friendly way they had welcomed us both. They seemed to remember the COA workers as their friends and as people who had tried to help them, in spite of what must have been to them the COAers' strange ways and words.

Lil told them that we had to leave now and begin our trip back to Constantine. That was the signal for the protests to begin. We could not stay for such a short time, they said. It was not possible. Besides, there was a grand *fête* tonight and tomorrow—a wedding. They remembered how intrigued my parents had been by the wedding celebration they'd seen, and they were sure I should take part in this one.

At last Lil said to me, "I really can't stay. I have a number of things for classes I need to get done before spring vacation is over. If you want to, you could stay, though, and I'll drive down again tomorrow afternoon to pick you up."

I didn't know what to say. When I couldn't visit a Kabyle village, I had wanted very much to see one. Now I had a chance to see Chaouia life, as few outsiders ever had. But what about the stories I'd heard my parents tell about all the fleas and lice among the people, about their dirtiness (dirtiness at least partly because of the difficulties in getting water, but still dirtiness)? What about the fact that I would hardly be able to talk to anyone—it would be only my few words of French to someone who didn't know much more, with a "la-bess" or two thrown in. What should I do?

This would probably be my only trip to my native land, and somehow I knew I would always regret it if I didn't do and see as much as I could while I was here. So in spite of being afraid and uncertain, I said I would like to stay. We went with Lil to her car. She took a blanket from the back seat. "Here, you can use this to sleep on. They may not have extras, and besides you'll know this one doesn't have any little 'visitors' on it."

I tried to make my goodbye to her casual and not gaze longingly after her car as it disappeared down the trail.

I never regretted deciding to stay—at least not for any of the reasons which had made me doubtful about it at first. Mebareka and Salim's house, possibly because she had worked in the clinic, was cleaner than most of the others around. It must have taken constant effort on her part to keep it that way and to keep her children as neat and clean as they were.

The language problem turned out to be not so bad as I'd feared either. Their oldest child was Halima, a girl a few years younger than I. She was in school and knew a little more French than I. So we could at least begin to understand each other. But we couldn't talk about anything complicated. We couldn't laugh and share together.

But to get back to when Lil was leaving. It was Halima who distracted me so that even before Lil was out of sight, I had forgotten about her. Halima did it by leading me into the courtyard of the house next to theirs. The people there were her relatives, of course, but I never did figure out exactly how they were related.

Two of the women and several of the children I recognized. They had been part of the group which had swarmed to greet us when we first arrived. Now they were busy at work. One woman, seated on the ground, was forming a clay bowl with her hands. Beside her were objects she had already made. One was a large round platter with low sides which came to points at four places. I found out the next morning how this kind of platter was used. I'll let you wait till then, too, to learn what it was used for.

Some of the clay containers were dry. A girl was polishing and smoothing them, one at a time. Her polishing tool was a snail shell which she rubbed carefully over the surface. Then she shook out the fine dust which was the result of her rubbing. Another woman was painting designs on the pieces that were already dried and polished. For a brush she used a twig with its ends finely split. The paint looked like dark, thinned mud. She was making designs, mostly crisscrossed lines which formed triangle shapes.

The potter had finished the bowl she was making and set it aside to dry. Now she beckoned to me. I followed her outside the courtyard and around the side of the house. There she pointed to a small circular wall of stones about a foot and a half high. It looked like the inside was filled with burnt grass and twigs. With her hand she brushed away this layer of charred ashes and one by one lifted out a bowl, a sort of pitcher, and another bigger, flatter bowl. Sometimes I'm not too quick to catch on to things, but even I realized this was the homemade kiln where she baked her pottery. Halima had come along, too, and her halting explanations fit in with what I had figured out.

The woman held the pitcher toward me. I took it carefully. In some spots it was blackened from the fire. It was orange-red and solid, and the dark brown painted crisscrosses went neatly around it.

"It's very nice. I like it," I said, hoping my smile and tone of voice would tell her what I meant, even if she couldn't understand the words. It wasn't until I tried to give it back to her that I realized she wanted me to keep it as a gift. I protested. But I could tell she really wanted me to have it . . . and I really wanted it.

Now when I look at it, it makes everything come back. It reminds me of the friendliness and hospitality of the people and of the simple beauty of their faraway valley. I think of the green wheat, the blue-gray mountains, the yellow-brown stone houses. It was part of this earth that had been used to make my pitcher. And so, because of my pitcher, I can never forget this valley and its people. They are always with me.

I didn't realize all this then. I just knew I had a souvenir that I liked very much. Clutching it in my hand, I went with Halima to the next house.

Squish-slap. Squish-slap. What could be making that strange sound? When we came to the courtyard doorway, I *saw* what it was, but I still

78

didn't *know* what it was.

Three sticks about three feet high were tied together at the top to form a tripod. From this tripod were hanging two cords and fastened to them was an animal skin (goat or sheep, I supposed). One cord was tied to where the front legs would have been, and the other to the back legs. Sitting by the tripod was a woman, her hand on the "back-legs" cord, which she pulled toward her, then pushed it away, back and forth, back and forth. And it was the liquid inside the skin which squished and slapped as the skin continued its steady forward and backward movement. Do you know what this woman was doing, what this "machine" was? For anyone who's not good at figuring such things out, she was churning butter.

I longed to talk to her, to ask her about the butter. But I couldn't. Not being able to communicate is quite frustrating, I found out.

Months later, back in the States, my folks had a professor friend of theirs, an anthropologist, at our home for dinner. (In case your dictionary isn't handy, an anthropologist is a scientist who studies the history of different groups of people and how their customs developed.) From looking at my pitcher, from hearing about the other things we'd observed, and from seeing some of my parents' pictures, he thought many of the Chaouia habits and customs had not changed much since the late stone age, thousands of years ago.

Of course they have transistor radios now, and women's dresses and scarves are made of nylon and other new fabrics. There were even a few cars around, and electricity had arrived in the village, if not at the mechtas. I had to wonder. How long would their old ways continue? Would the young people have the time or the desire to learn the old ways?

After watching the butter churner, we went back to Mebareka's and a supper of *couscous*. I had eaten it before, since Mother loves to fix it, but you may not know what I'm talking about. Couscous is the main food across North Africa, along with bread. It is made from wheat flour and meal moistened and rolled through screen sieves until little balls are formed. These tiny balls are the couscous.

It's cooked in special double-decker pots. The bottom pot contains boiling water or soup and the top one, which has holes in its bottom to let the steam enter, contains the couscous grains, which steam until tender. It can be eaten with a meat and vegetable soup poured over it, or with sour milk, or with a tomato sauce minus other vegetables and meat. Or you can sweeten it with sugar and add raisins to it.

This time we simply had it with tomato sauce, and we all used our spoons to help ourselves from one bowl in the middle of the little table. A bit of warm water to rinse the couscous pot, the bowl, the spoons, and our coffee cups from the afternoon, and our dishes were done.

Then I went with Mebareka and Halima to see the first stage of the wedding celebrations. This was at the bride's home. She was a Maanser, of course, and Halima's cousin. And she was my age! This wasn't unusual. After about age twelve, girls are shut up at home until time to be married. So Halima would soon stop going to school, if her parents followed the customs of the mechta.

The bride was not marrying a Maanser, so she would be leaving the mechta the next day to go to her husband's home. Now she looked sad. She was sitting on the floor, and heaped around her in display, were all the dresses which her in-laws had delivered that day as a part of their payment of her parents. Some of the dresses were bright-flowered nylon prints. Others were of finer material with designs stitched in gold and silver thread.

The room was packed with women and girls who were singing a rhythmic chant as they watched an old woman pounding a mortar stone in time with their chant. I didn't know then what she was grinding, but could see it was some kind of dried leaves being turned into a powder. When enough of these leaves had been crushed, water was added to form a thick paste.

When I saw them apply this paste to the soles of the bride's feet and to the palms of her hands, I remembered. My parents had described *henna,* and I knew this was it.

I eagerly offered my right hand, too, to have the paste applied when they asked if I wished to have some. I thought I would feel like a real Algerian then. After the paste was rubbed on, I made my hand into a fist, and they wrapped a cloth around it, so that none of the dye would touch anything else.

The singing and chanting continued through most of the night, but we left after an hour, I suppose for my benefit. Back at our house, Mebareka immediately unbound my hand, took some of their precious supply of water, and rinsed off the paste. My palm had already turned a warm orange-brown color which would gradually vanish only after many days and many washings. My thumbnail, the only nail to be dyed because it had been inside my fist, would keep its henna color until the nail had completely grown out.

This dye is thought to make a person more beautiful and to bring good luck and good health. It is often used during Muslim holidays and for local fêtes and marriages. Many use it to dye their hair also. It makes the hair beautiful and discourages lice, they think.

When we got home, the family's several sheep and goats and one cow had been brought into the courtyard. They were standing under a roof which extended from the courtyard wall to form a rough stable. Since the weather was nice, Halima and I laid our blankets on the ground in the courtyard also, opposite the stable and the little fenced-in corner where the chickens were penned up for the night.

Lying on the hard ground with the animals nearby, I wondered if the place where Jesus had been born had been something like this. With this thought I was soon asleep.

Dressing in the morning was no problem, because we hadn't undressed. I had a comb in my shoulder bag to take care of my hair, and washing up was just a splash of water on my face and hands from a tin basin.

Breakfast preparation was already underway. Above a little fire, a large four-pointed clay platter sat on three rocks. It was just like the one I'd seen the potter making. Mebarcka mixed some meal with water and a little salt and kneaded the sticky mass together. Then she pressed it flat and round to about one inch thick and fifteen inches wide.

Halima placed this bread dough on the hot clay baking dish, and we sat watching it bake. From time to time she added a piece of fuel to the fire. The fuel was dried cow "chips" (manure). This might sound strange, but what would you suggest they use? They tried to save some of this to use on their fields as fertilizer, but for the daily baking, it was about the only thing available.

This morning I took more notice of the two younger children. Little sister Hadda, about five years old, busily played with her dolls while breakfast was being prepared. Her dolls were two sticks fastened together in the shape of a cross for the body and arms. They were dressed in scraps of old clothing. Like all the other girls and women, Hadda's ears were pierced, but either she wasn't old enough for the huge silver earrings the women wore, or else she had some which weren't for every day. So what she wore in each ear to keep the hole open was a large-size safety-pin!

Hocine was the youngest, a two-year old boy. He still wore a dress, as all the little boys do. He had a bare bottom, which meant there were no stacks of diapers to wash.

Around his neck, like a necklace, hung a little leather pouch on a string. I tried to ask what this was. Mebareka and Halima together managed to explain that inside it was a verse from the Koran written by a *marabout* (mare-ah-boo) or holy man. This was supposed to help keep Hocine well and keep evil away. I was surprised that someone who'd worked in a clinic would believe in such things. Still, that year of clinic work had been only a small part of Mebareka's life. And I remembered the way some people think of rabbits' feet and fourleaf clovers, and realized I had better not be too critical.

Halima placed the bread dough on the hot clay baking dish, and we sat watching it bake.

After the bread had been browned on both sides and taken from the fire, everyone broke off a hunk. It was warm, solid, and filling. Along with some coffee, this was our breakfast.

Then we were ready to join the other Maansers who were starting to walk through the fields to the groom's house in a neighboring mechta a mile away. Today's wedding celebrations would take place there. The bride had already left in an old car borrowed for the occasion. Another car and a pickup truck followed, all of them loaded with relatives. The vehicles honked wildly as the small procession transported the bride to her new home.

As we walked along, we passed a field which was even rockier than most of the others. When I looked closer, I saw that the stones were not just lying there, but were grouped in low mounds. On each mound two or three of the stones stood upright. Mebareka must have noticed me staring.

"It is the field of the dead people," she explained in her best French. Then I understood—it was a cemetery.

"Two stones standing up," she said as she pointed where a stone was upright at each end of a mound, "is a man. Three stones is a woman."

There were no names—nor anything else—other than the two or three standing stones, to make one grave different from another. My French wasn't good enough to ask about this, but I supposed they would remember where a person was buried by the location.

When we arrived at the groom's home, we took our segregated places in the crowd. Women, girls, and small children sat together under a canopy of bright-colored blankets by the house. The bride and the other young women of marriageable age and those married but still young were inside the house and out of sight of the eyes of the men. The men and boys were standing in a large semicircle, with the house and the women at the open end.

I wondered when the wedding would take place. Later I found out that it never did. That is, there is no wedding ceremony or service, as we think of it, but once the bride arrives at her new home, the couple is considered married.

I did see other ceremonies, though. One or two men danced around the center of the circle and shot off their guns in what looked like a careless and dangerous way. No one was shot, so maybe it wasn't as dangerous as it seemed.

Between ceremonies some musicians (men) performed. Two played wooden flutes and one held a drum. He held it vertically (like a bass drum) and beat out a complicated rhythm with his fingers. The music seemed to repeat over and over, with only a few different notes. While they played, they also sang and danced in slow backward and forward steps. And apparently they asked for money, because from time to time someone in the audience offered a bill, which was then displayed and commented on. As near as I could tell, the musicians kept some of this money, and some of it went to the young couple. Perhaps this was their way of doing what we do when we give wedding or shower gifts and display them afterward.

Then Halima went to join some other girls about

her age who were getting ready to dance in the center of the circle. One of them sat down to tap out the rhythm on the drum, and the other girls and women began to sing—a sing-song chant which repeated the same sad (at least to me it sounded sad) tune over and over. I wished I could understand the words. Was it sad? Or was it happy? Was it a special wedding song and dance? I never found out.

The five dancers were side by side, all of them making the three movements of their dance at the same time. Their feet made quick little steps, backward and forward. In their hands they held nylon scarves which they swirled and waved up and down and around. But the strangest movement and the most remarkable one was their stomachs jerking up and down in rhythm with the music.

I wish I could show you a movie of it. It still seems impossible to me. Just try to move that part of your body up and down. I guarantee you won't be able to. In and out, yes, but up and down?

When I asked Halima afterward how she did it, she laughed and said, "It is very easy," but she could not explain how she did it. I think she must have learned it when she was very young.

I enjoyed observing all these new things and knew I was lucky to have come here the day a wedding was going on. But after a couple of hours, I had seen what there was to see. I wasn't able to talk to anyone or to understand what they were saying to each other or what the music was saying. I wasn't able to joke with anyone about the things that struck me as strange or funny. By the end of another half hour I was becoming restless, and wondering how much longer we would stay and how many hours it would be till Lil would come back to pick me up.

Then it was time to eat—couscous with meat, and some warm orange soda. I was glad for the soda. My stomach was beginning to feel unsteady and would probably have rebelled at any more strong coffee.

Perhaps it was because of the music that I hadn't heard a car drive up, so I was surprised when I glanced up from my food to see a newcomer in the circle of men, someone I recognized. It was Carl, that neat-looking COA teacher who had been at Lil's the other evening. He must have just arrived because he was greeting and being greeted by several of the men. The men's usual greeting is to shake hands, then place their hand over their heart. I saw him point toward me and then he began to make his way around the circle to where I was sitting among the women and girls.

"Hi," he said. "Hope you don't mind that I came to pick you up instead of Lil. Are you ready to leave?"

I was about to nod yes when they brought some food to him, which he couldn't refuse.

"This is really interesting," he said, glancing around as he was eating. "Till now I haven't had any contact with the Chaouia people. But we should get going as soon as possible."

"Why? I mean I'm ready to go, but I hadn't expected Lil till later on today. And how did you find me?"

"Lil told me how to find the mechta, but I must admit I was a bit shocked to find the place almost deserted. It made me think of your experience in Algiers! But there were a couple of kids around who finally were able to make me understand that everyone had gone to a wedding and pointed me in this direction. I've got to get at least a few pictures of this before we leave," he said, and quickly took some shots.

"Ready?" he asked afterward.

Following five minutes of farewells and thank-yous and as many kisses as had welcomed me the day before, we were ready to go.

"What's my suitcase doing here?" I asked as I climbed into his car. There it was, in the back seat!

"Did you leave anything at the mechta?".

"No," I said. For some reason I had stuck the pitcher in my shoulder bag before we walked to the wedding that morning. "Oh, wait. I did leave Lil's blanket there. But why have you got my suitcase?"

"The blanket won't matter. I'll explain as soon as we get going," he said. But he didn't say anything at all as he concentrated on following the jouncing track which wandered through the fields and down across a dry stream bed, and finally onto a black-topped road.

"Now," he said. "Lil couldn't come for you because she's been expelled from the country."

"What? That can't be true!"

"But it is. Late yesterday afternoon when she returned to Constantine, they were waiting for her. The officials told her she had to be ready to leave on the first flight this morning."

"But why? Does it have anything to do with what happened in Algiers?" I felt it might somehow be my fault. She had come there to get me that morning.

"I don't think there's a connection. There's probably no real reason. She's been here quite awhile and they may not want any foreigners to be here long enough to be so well liked as she is. What they told her was that she was a 'subversive influence' on the students. I think they've been checking closely on her since she picked you up at the Palmeraie. Or maybe even before that—since they questioned her the first time."

"When did she leave?"

"She was luckier than the Algiers folks. She didn't have to leave immediately. We worked most of the night helping her decide what to do with her furniture and household goods. She could take only two suitcases with her. We packed a trunk of the other things she wanted most to keep and sent that off this morning. I hope it'll go through okay. Everything else she had to leave behind.

"Well, she was quite concerned about you. There was no way to let you know, and it wouldn't have helped anyway. We thought of coming for you last night and having you leave with her this morning. But you've got some time left yet, and I'm heading back to Ghardaia, so I said I could take you along there—that way you'll see some of the Sahara Desert. From there you can fly to Algiers and be on your way home. So that's the reason for the suitcase. I hope you'll think this is a good plan, because there's not much else you can do now!"

91

I felt kind of sick. How had she felt, having to leave her home and friends? And as for me, the one person I really knew was gone. I was sure Carl was okay, or Lil wouldn't have agreed to let me go with him, but he was almost a stranger. And what would I do for money?

"I'd love to see the desert," I said slowly. "But I don't think I have enough money for an extra plane ticket. Or to spend traveling."

"Don't worry. I'd be coming this way anyway and buying my gas. Meals won't be much. And the fare from Ghardaia to Algiers probably won't be much different than from Constantine to Algiers. We'll just trade in that part of your ticket. The only thing I'm concerned about is that the police don't decide to suspect me of something because I'm a friend of Lil's. I'd like to finish out my term here. They did pull in Malika too and questioned her about where she'd been with Lil and why."

"How about me?" I asked.

"You?"

"Yes. I've been with her everywhere they've been following her."

"I think they did ask her about you. But they ought to know you're a tourist. They can check where your visa was issued, if they have any doubts. And they know you're nothing but a harmless, underaged kid who sleeps through everything and doesn't know what the score is!" he joked.

I wasn't convinced.

"I'm not sure how much time we should take for sight-seeing along the way," he continued. "Timgad, which is a large city of Roman ruins, wouldn't

92

be out of our way. We're heading for Biskra. Take a look on the map."

I looked and saw where we were, east of Ain M'Lila and heading south.

"It's up to you," I said. "I've seen Djemilla already."

"We'll skip Timgad then, if you've already seen some ruins. I stopped to see it on my way up north. I am interested in seeing El Oued, though—southeast of Biskra" (he pointed on the map). "Then till we head across the Sahara to Ghardaia, it'll be almost time for me to be back at school, and for you to start home. By the way, Lil said she'll call your folks as soon as she's in the States, probably sometime today, and let them know what's happened and that you're in good hands."

By then it was about noon and plenty warm. For the rest of the day we would be going south, and probably the temperature would become warmer and warmer as we went. The route we were taking went right through the town of Timgad. We got there in about an hour, and it looked like any other village, but as we drove by, I could see some of the ruins jutting up behind the hills. From what was visible I thought it might have been an even larger place than Djemila.

But I soon forgot Timgad when I saw what was coming toward us. Partly on the road, and partly spread across the field beside the road, was a large caravan of camels. Carl stopped the car, and we got out so he could try to talk to the people and take a few pictures. It was a group of Sahara nomads coming north as they do every year, to escape from the desert summer and find grazing for their animals.

There must have been at least fifty camels plus some sheep and goats. The people were walking rather than riding, but the caravan was moving at such a slow pace that it was easy for them to keep up. Only a few of the camels were needed to carry the nomads' possessions—their household equipment and their folded-up tent homes.

But one kingly-looking camel, covered with brightly colored striped blankets, had a different job. Some of the blankets were stretched over a frame to form a canopy, and sitting in the shade of this "camel cabin" was a young woman with a small baby. She smiled and waved to us. Then the caravan was past, continuing its plodding path north. We got back into our car to race on south into the wilderness from which they had come.

As we went, the countryside became more desolate. We were getting into a rocky, mountainous region. Soon there were no more green fields to soothe our eyes—only glaring rocks. This place was so barren and the sun so bright, it made me wonder if we weren't already in the desert. Carl assured me that we wouldn't really be in the Sahara until we had passed through the mountains.

Two routes lead to Biskra, the first city on the desert side of the mountains. We were taking the smaller, less-traveled one. There was not too much traffic, particularly now during the heat of the day. So when we saw a parking place along the side of the road with several cars pulled off and with people gazing from a lookout point, we stopped, too, to see what was so interesting.

Below us was a deep canyon. There must have

been a stream at its bottom, because palms were growing thickly there. Their green was a cooling change from the glare of the rocks. I was sure it was an oasis, even if this spot was not officially a part of the Sahara!

"That's not what everyone's looking at," Carl said when he realized I was still looking at the trees. "Look straight across the canyon, up higher."

When I finally saw the houses, I wasn't surprised I hadn't noticed them before. They were built into the canyon sides. The canyon had been formed in such a way that near the top its sides were in steps, with narrow ledges on different heights. On each ledge were houses. They were nearly invisible because of being built from the same rocks as the canyon. It reminded me of the old Indian cliff dwellings in the western United States. But these houses in Rhouffi, as the place was called, were still lived-in homes.

From there we were soon out of the mountains and arriving at Biskra.

When we stopped for gas, I had a few minutes to look around. Gigantic palms lined the streets and cooled them with their leafy shadows. Behind the trees, white walls were set in the sandy orange earth, guarding from view the homes behind them. What I couldn't see was what I wanted to see. How did the people behind the walls live—like the Chaouia? Or like the people of Constantine? Or in some completely different way?

But Carl wanted to go on. "Biskra isn't all that interesting compared to what's still ahead," he said. "We're barely on the edge of the desert here."

The further south we went, the more disappointed I became. There were no lovely rolling sand dunes, just dry stony ground with a few ugly looking bushes, and once in awhile the humpy shapes of camels ambling slowly across the background. It was boring.

The places marked as towns on the map were so small that we were through them before I realized it. At least there was no chance to get lost in them, I thought. There was only one road, and we were on it! Everything looked so much the same that I almost wondered if we were moving. But watching the edge of the road whiz by and feeling the hot air pushing against my face convinced me that we were.

By then I was starved and glad to find out that Carl had bought some bread, cheese, and dates (which Biskra is famous for) when we'd stopped for gas. We drank from the thermos of water he'd brought along from Constantine that morning.

Then it was dark, and we still had a ways to go to El Oued. "Where are we going to sleep?" I asked.

"Oh, we'll stop along here somewhere," Carl replied.

And we did. I found that camping in the desert is simple. All we did was pull off the road and out of sight behind a dune. Carl spread his sleeping bag on the sand beside the car, and I stretched out as comfortably as I could on the back seat.

People told us later that we had done a dangerous thing, that we might easily have been robbed. Either we were lucky or else those reports of thieves roaming the desert were exaggerated.

I couldn't believe it when I sat up in the morning and looked out the car window. Sand, sky, and sun were pale in the early morning light, but this was the desert of my dreams. Dunes, dunes, dunes every direction I looked—each one an individual wind sculpture. Some were rounded with graceful ripples covering their surface. Others swept smoothly to a point, like giant waves, frozen just as they were about to break.

I noticed Carl's sleeping bag was rolled up, and some tracks led from where he'd been lying, off into the dunes. I used a bit of the water still left in the thermos to wipe off my face and hands, and ate a couple of the dates left from the day before.

Then I saw Carl coming around a dune. He put his sleeping bag in the car, locked it, and said, "Come on. Let me show you what I found."

It wasn't so easy to walk through all that sand, as you can imagine if you've ever been on a beach. We went around a couple of dunes, then began climbing one. What a surprise when we got to the top, and I looked down to see a house and some date palms below. I had imagined we were miles and miles from anyone else. But there beneath us was a tiny oasis sitting at the bottom of a sand bowl. Walls of sand rose on all sides of the little domed house so that it was completely hidden if you were below the dune.

We were standing on the top rim of the bowl, and all around this rim, palm branches were stuck in

We thanked the man at the little farm at the bottom of the dune for the drink he gave us, even though it tasted awful.

the ground. "They're like a snow fence," Carl said. "I was talking to the guy down there. Even with this 'fence,' they spend a lot of time hauling back up the sand which keeps seeping down on them. It seems as though there are a lot of little farms like this around El Oued."

We went down inside the bowl, and I saw they had a well and were growing a few vegetables besides their date palms. The farmer was getting water from his well and dumping it into a small trough which ran into a ditch and then into more ditches among the rows of vegetables. Carl helped him pull down a long pole which rested on another pole—like a giant seesaw. As the one end went down, the other, having a cord attached to it, came up, pulling with it the skin full of water from the well. Letting the pole down would send the skin tumbling into the well for more water.

We thanked him for the drink he gave us, even though it tasted awful. I hoped the vegetables liked it better than I did.

Then we went back to the car. The sun was higher now, and turned the sand to a bright light brown. The fantastic shapes of the dunes were even clearer than before, outlined against the bright blue sky.

It wasn't far to El Oued, a city I'll always remember—for several reasons. The first reason was the domes everywhere. Each house, sometimes each room, had a domed roof. Not surprisingly, it's called "The City of a Thousand Domes." Among these thousands of curving white domes were more thousands of dark green curves—the branches of

100

date palms. And the two together made the city something to see.

We looked at some of the things for sale. I didn't think I could spare much money because I hadn't known I would get to the desert and had bought too many things in Constantine. But I wanted to buy at least one thing as a reminder of my trip through the desert. Finally I decided on something for less than a dollar—a camel muzzle woven from palm fibers. Hanging on a wall, it would look like a plant holder.

My other reason for remembering El Oued occurred when we were leaving a little restaurant where we'd gotten something to eat before starting off again.

We were standing near the door to pay our bill when a small white dog wandered in. The restaurant owner leaned over the counter and said something like, "Get out of here!" in Arabic, but the dog paid no attention. I was holding the newspaper which Carl had just bought, so I rolled it up and gave the dog a little whack on its rear, telling it to scram. It turned fiercely and sank its teeth into the paper. I was frightened, but before I could run, it had also sunk its teeth into my leg.

About that time two men came in shouting (as I learned later), "Has anyone seen a white dog? Be careful. It has just bitten two people!"

By then the dog had left, so everyone took after it while I stood there, bleeding.

Carl was soon back, looking angry. "Of all things, they killed the dog while we were trying to capture it!"

"Well, I guess they shouldn't have, but I can't bring myself to feel too sorry for it," I said. "I'll never believe it now when someone says dogs will leave you alone if you show you're not scared of them."

"That's not the point," Carl said. "If the dog's dead, we can't watch it to see if it had rabies or not."

"Rabies!" I didn't know exactly what that was, but I found out later it's a disease which is always fatal (only one person has ever been known to survive it). The way to prevent it is to take a series of fourteen shots so painful and dangerous that people don't want to take them unless they know for sure that the animal that's bitten them had rabies. Now the dog was dead. What would we do?

Carl was discussing the situation with the men who had helped catch (and kill) the dog. They finally decided to put the dead dog in a box tied to the top of our car and take along the man who was bitten and the father of the boy who was bitten, and head for Touggourt, where there was a veterinarian who they hoped might be able to tell us what to do.

Carl got out a little first-aid kit from his car and cleaned and bandaged my bite and those of the man and boy. While he was doing this, several other men wearing gloves carefully put the dog in a box and onto the car roof. Apparently if an animal had rabies, it could be dangerous even to touch its body. Any saliva on the body might give rabies to the person touching it, if he had a cut or put his finger to his mouth, or something like that.

My leg throbbed and I was almost too shook up to

enjoy the scenery we were passing through on our way to Touggourt. There were more fabulous dunes with little villages and groups of palm trees scattered here and there. Then we were out of the dunes and in a region of rocky sand again. When I looked back after awhile, I could still see the dunes. Now they looked like distant golden mountains on the horizon.

At last we arrived at Touggourt, a larger town than El Oued. We were fortunate to find there really was a vet there and that he wasn't on vacation or out somewhere on a call.

I went along to the vet's office. Since I didn't understand much of the conversation, Carl explained to me afterward what happened. The vet said there was no way he could know whether the dog had had rabies or not. The only place to find out was at the Institut Pasteur in Algiers (named after Louis Pasteur, the French scientist who in 1885 found out how to give shots to prevent rabies).

You will not believe what the vet's solution was. He cut off the dog's head, packed it in ice, and sent his assistant by the next plane to Algiers with this little "icebox." There some of the dog's brain would be injected into mice. If the mice got rabies, we would know the dog had had it. And guess who paid for this man's trip to Algiers. Me. Except that I didn't have the money, so Carl paid it and I promised him that my parents would pay him back.

"The vet thinks it will be three or four days till the lab work is finished," Carl told me, "so I made it as plain as I could that they'll need to send two reports—one to me at Ghardaia, which is where

103

we'll be by then, and the other to the people in El Oued who were bitten." (After the vet had done his bit, the two men who had come with us from El Oued went back there by bus, since we were going on further south.)

"How soon . . . does a person get rabies?" I asked. "I mean if the dog really had rabies, how soon do the shots have to begin?" I was thinking of the four days we had to wait yet.

"If you'd been bitten on the face or neck, it would be more serious—the farther from the brain the bite is, the longer it takes rabies to develop. But it's usually at least three weeks. The vet doesn't think we need to worry. But I'll check with the doctor in Ghardaia as soon as we get there," he reassured me.

It was late afternoon by the time all this was taken care of. We ate in a restaurant again so we could use the restrooms, such as they were, and so we could get cleaned up a bit. The restroom had indoor plumbing but no stool—just a hole to squat over with a place on both sides to put your feet. When flushing this kind I discovered you should pull the chain and run, because water is likely to come pouring over the whole thing. Actually, after having used bushes, rocks, and dunes the last few days, I thought this more modern thing was quite nice.

Carl filled the thermos with bottled water for drinking and bought some bread for breakfast, and we drove on south a ways before stopping for another night under the desert sky.

During the night it was cool, but once the sun came up, the coolness was suddenly gone. Soon the ground became so hot from the direct and burning sun that heat was hitting us from two directions— above and below. As we headed still further south, it became almost hard to breath. The air blowing in the open windows was so hot it almost smothered us. Its dryness sucked the moisture from our bodies, and I couldn't keep away from the thermos. Even though the water in it tasted warm and stale, it moistened my parched lips.

Mile after mile the desert slid by us, each mile the same as the one before—unchanging, barren, and hot. Then on the horizon, a flame burst above the sand, and the temperature seemed to rise still higher. We were approaching Hassi Messaoud, one of the Sahara oil fields. As we came closer, we could see several of these flames, burning off the extra gas from the wells, and the black smoke from them swept up across the blue sky.

When we came still nearer, the roar of their burning sounded like a huge locomotive.

The town itself was fenced in, and was off limits to visitors. So we had only an outside-the-fence view of a group of modern buildings, built somewhere else and plunked down here as homes for the oil workers. The swimming pools we glimpsed showed that these workers were well taken care of. Carl said he'd heard they were so well paid they could have whatever they wanted brought in by plane. Plus every few weeks they could leave their hot desert prison and fly north for several days.

"Hassi Messaoud is a strange kind of oasis," Carl said. "It doesn't exist because of water, like the old oases, but because of something else just about as necessary today as water—oil."

Hassi was the farthest south we went, so it was hard for me to believe what I saw when I checked where it was on the map. After several days of going south into the desert, we were still less than a third of the way from the Mediterranean Sea to Algeria's most southern tip. Or if I counted only the Sahara part of Algeria, we had not gone even a fifth of the length of the desert in our journey south to Hassi.

From there we angled slightly north but mostly west, on our way toward Carl's home base of Ghardaia. After a medium-sized town called Ouargla, it was more miles of dreary sameness—always the same scenery and always the same intense heat. I thought, "This is what a cake or a pizza must feel like in an oven—heat pushing in at you from all directions."

There was one small restaurant-store along that route. It showed what the saying "out in the middle of nowhere" means. But even in the middle of nowhere, the building had a Coke sign on the front, and we stopped to get out of the sun a few minutes and have a drink.

"I guess I should tell you a little about Ghardaia before we get there," Carl said as we were leaving the café. "The people there are a Berber tribe, the Mozabites, and—"

"Another Berber tribe?" I interrupted.

He looked at me questioningly.

"Well, first I heard about the Kabyles. Then it was the Chaouia. Now the Mozabites?"

"Yes," Carl said. "But these people are different from the others, although their language is similar. They're Muslims, but a different kind. They're from a small strict group which began soon after the time of Muhammad. This group thinks all the other Muslims are wrong. Way back in history they fought with other groups and finally fled into the desert. This was about a thousand years ago. By digging over 3000 wells, many more than 200 feet deep, they've created seven small cities where before there was nothing.

"Because they can't make a living in the desert, the men take turns going north for two years," Carl continued. "Then they come back to their desert homeland. They're mostly shopkeepers, and lots of the stores in the northern cities, especially grocery stores, are owned by Mozabites. They're exceptionally clean and honest people, and also very strict—no tobacco, no games, no music.

"Some Arabs live in their cities, but the Mozabites look down on them as second-class people, good only for servants," Carl concluded.

So I knew a bit about the people, but when we arrived, the sight of their towns surprised me. All at once, there they were in the midst of desolate, rocky hills. The seven towns all looked alike, but different from the other desert towns I'd seen. In other towns, everything was white. Here the houses were a delicate blue. Not along the streets, though. There, as always, I saw only blank walls. Most of these were the orange-brown color of the sandy earth they came from. But looking down on one of the towns from the nearby hills, I could see

108

the open courtyards of the houses. And nearly all these courtyard walls were painted in tints of blue.

Each town also had its mosque, built on the highest part of the town. Again, all the minarets were alike, but different from those of mosques in other places. They were simple and unadorned, not painted or whitewashed, and had no balconies around the tops. They were wider at the bottom, tapering off at the top. Their shape reminded me of the John Hancock Tower in Chicago. The top came to four points on the four corners, with an open half-moon window in the center of each side.

The blue houses and the unusual mosques gave Ghardaia and her sister towns a special character of their own.

It was late afternoon as we drove into town. Carl said we'd go to the doctor first. If we couldn't see him, then we'd arrange a time for the next day. After a wait of over an hour, we did get in.

The first thing he did was give me a tetanus shot, which he said I should have had right away. Otherwise, he said, "Don't worry about waiting a day or so more. If you find you need the anti-rabies serum, I'll get you a prescription and you can get it filled at the pharmacy. Then I can give the shots."

When we left the office, I said, "But fourteen shots, one a day! I can't stay here two weeks!"

"Don't worry. He can get you started. Then, if your trip home takes more than one day, we'll arrange somehow to have you get one on the way."

From the doctor's office we went to Carl's apartment on the edge of town where the non-Mozabites lived.

"Do you get lonely here?" I asked. "Or don't you mind being away from the other COA people? Are there any other Americans around?"

"To the last question, no there aren't. To the first question, yes, I get lonely sometimes. During the day and some evenings I'm busy with school work, but it would be nice to have someone to talk things over with," Carl admitted. "The first year I was here, a COA couple taught in the same school, and that was great. But it was the last year of their term, and no one came to replace them, so this year I'm on my own. I spend some time writing to my girl friend. She came for a visit at the end of my first year. So she's seen what it's like, and that makes it easier for me to write to her."

"Could you ask to be somewhere else if you wanted to?" I asked.

"I don't really want to, but even if I did, it probably wouldn't change anything," Carl said. "All the high school teachers are assigned to their schools by the government education office in Algiers, and there's not much choice as to where you go. This is an interesting place, and I don't regret being here. But it's hard to get to know any of the Mozabites very well. They're not open to outsiders."

Not long after we had arrived at the apartment, there was a knock at the door. Carl opened it.

"Oh, hi there, Hakim," he said. "Come on in. How's it going in Algiers?"

And in he came, an Algerian who looked like he was maybe a few years younger than Carl.

"Hakim was one of my English students last year, and this year he's at the university in Algiers," Carl explained.

I wondered how he was going to explain me to Hakim.

"And this is Zina, born in Algeria of American parents. She's here on a visit to see what her native land is like. I met her at the friend's I was visiting in Constantine. When my friend had to leave suddenly, I offered to bring Zina along and show her the desert on my way back here."

Hakim looked very interested. "Who was this friend and what do you mean, 'had to leave suddenly'?"

Carl hesitated, not sure how much he should say.

"Carl, I want to know," Hakim insisted. "Is this

111

friend a Christian? Did he need to leave because of being a Christian?"

"It was a *she,* and yes, I think being a Christian had something to do with it. She'd been here about seventeen years. Why do you ask?"

"Do you know about the Christians in Algiers who were expelled?"

"Yes!" I said without thinking.

"Oh!" He looked at me. "I think I can guess. Are you the girl who slept through the raid?"

"Good grief," I thought. "Is that story known all over the country?"

Carl laughed. "You're right. But how do you know about it, Hakim?"

"I'll tell you. That's why I came to see you right away. I've been watching for you ever since I got home from Algiers a few days ago. You remember last year, a couple of times, I asked you what it really means to be a Christian, and why you came here?"

"Sure, I remember."

"This year in Algiers I found the student center you told me about, where you can study or read the Bible and talk. I'm learning more about Christianity, and I think it is the true way," Hakim said thoughtfully. "Anyway, a friend from the university invited me to go with him to that weekend gathering at the Palmeraie. I didn't have time to go because I was getting ready to come home for vacation. But I saw him afterward—after the police let him go. He knows I am interested in Christianity, and he told me to stay away from it, to keep away from Christians. He said the police want him and

112

the others to spy on any Algerians they think may
be Christians, and on all the missionaries they
know. If they don't cooperate, they may lose their
jobs or be kicked out of the university. And he
thinks he and the rest are being spied on
themselves, that they are being followed wherever
they go."

"He's probably telling you the truth," Carl said.
"What do you think about it?"

"It worries me," Hakim replied. "To be able to
have a good job, I need to finish university. If I became a Christian, that could make it very difficult
for me. But from what you told me and from what I
studied, I think that Jesus is for everyone. I should
be able to be a Christian and a good Algerian at the
same time."

"You can be, Hakim," Carl assured him. "But
many people, including people from your government, don't understand that. They don't believe it's
possible. Your own family and friends probably
wouldn't understand either."

"What shall I do?"

"You're the one who has to decide that," Carl
said. "The best way I can help you is to pray for
you. I can't tell you what to do."

And Carl did pray with him, asking that Hakim
would want to find God's way for him and that God
would show him His help and love.

Then Carl said, "You may be in trouble already
for coming here to see me."

"Why?"

"Zina and I are under suspicion, just by being
foreign Christians. And not only was she with the

group in Algiers that got in trouble, but she and I were both with Lil Thomas, our friend who was expelled, shortly after that. I think they're keeping their eye on us."

"You never told me!" I exclaimed.

"Huh! Do you think I tell you everything I know?"

"You could at least have told me that. Here I was enjoying everything so much!"

"Exactly," Carl said. "Why shouldn't you be enjoying yourself? There wasn't any point in mentioning it. Maybe I shouldn't have now, either. But a couple of times along the way, I thought I saw that same fellow who was hanging around outside Lil's apartment that evening. He drives one of those big black Peugeots."

Ugh! Not old black car and blue shirt. I was glad I hadn't seen him.

Then Carl and Hakim went to the door. "Hakim, come back again before you leave for Algiers. If you think you should, that is, and have time to."

"I will, Carl. I think I have almost decided. I know it's something I have to make up my mind about soon."

I hardly knew what to think after he'd left. Lil had told me how difficult it is to be a Christian in Algeria, but now I knew an actual person who was facing this problem. From what I was used to hearing in church, becoming a Christian was a way to be happy and to have God be with you and take care of all your problems. But now I was learning that for some people, it is the way to find persecution and unhappiness. Dare to be a Christian in Algeria and

114

you may lose your job, your family, your friends.

I told Carl what I was thinking. "You're right but you're wrong," He said. "You may lose family and friends, but you gain new ones in the church. Maybe you misunderstood what you thought you heard in church. Being a Christian doesn't mean no more problems or difficulties—not for anyone, here or anywhere else. But what you have is a new way to face whatever there is, and a new Person to be with you in everything that comes along."

I sighed. Why was life so complicated?

I thought I should help Carl fix something to eat, but since my cooking experience didn't go beyond using mixes and opening cans and sticking things from the freezer into the oven, my skills were not too useful here.

It was late and we were too tired to go shopping, so we ate what was on hand—a packet of powdered soup which he prepared, and some cheese and fruit which were still in the tiny refrigerator from before he'd left.

The couch felt so good that I slept soundly. How many nights had it been since I'd slept on something this comfortable? Two nights I'd been scrunched up in the car, and the one before that I'd slept on the ground with Halima.

Now I was wide awake and it looked like the middle of the morning. The bedroom door was still shut, so I thought Carl must be having a good sleep too, back in his own bed again.

By the time I had used the bathroom for a good long shower and hair wash and was dressed, I heard Carl stirring around too.

"What do you want to do today?" he asked as we sat drinking *café au lait* (hot milk with a little coffee added) and eating some fresh bread that he had bought in a nearby shop. "If you know when you want to leave, we could go see about your reservations, and then do a little sight-seeing afterward."

"I think I'm ready to go anytime," I said, "I've seen and done so much already in the time I've been here. But I guess I'll have to wait for that report from Institut Pasteur, won't I?"

"Yeah. I'd forgotten that for the moment. This is the third day since it happened, and counting the time it took the vet's assistant to get there—it'll probably be at least a few more days till we hear."

By the time we'd finished our breakfast, it was lunchtime, but we set out on foot to see the sights. Many of the streets were too narrow for cars, and the town wasn't all that big anyway.

We went first to an open square, a sort of market area on the lower edge of town. Here a few cars and bikes and a van were parked. Some donkeys and camels stood nearby. Around the square were arch-covered walks with small shops tucked back under these arcades. I could tell that many of the people walking around and looking at the goods on display were tourists like me. Some were probably foreign teachers from the north using their school vacation to see the desert.

Hand-woven wool rugs and carpets were the most popular items on display. But besides these there were also handmade leather *poufs* (unstuffed hassocks) and brightly painted camel saddles.

I could soon tell the Mozabite men from the Arabs. The Mozabites had paler skin and rounder faces, and they didn't wear turbans on their heads. Instead they wore little white hats the shape and size of upside-down cereal bowls.

"Is Hakim a Mozabite?" I asked. Like most of the young men, he hadn't worn anything on his head.

"No, he's Arab. I haven't been able to get that friendly with any of the Mozabites."

Seeing us looking around, a man offered to show us their holy mosque. Carl had never been in it either, so we agreed to go with him. We left the square with the man in the lead and began a steady climb up the narrow winding street. Whenever I glanced up, I could see that mysterious pyramid-shaped minaret tower beckoning us on.

It was not the hour of prayer, so we were allowed to go in. The inside of the mosque was so simple I was almost disappointed. Plain straw mats covered the floor. There was no color, no design, no decoration of any kind, only the sunlight from the open courtyard making patterns on the whitewashed pillared archways and the walls.

There wasn't much more to see in Ghardaia, so Carl paid the guide, and we went back down the hill toward "home," stopping a couple of places to buy food for the evening meal. Carl bought a melon, a loaf of bread, some lettuce, a can of tomato paste, some spaghetti, and a half pound of hamburger.

Nothing except the can of tomato paste was pre-packaged. There were no styrofoam trays, plastic, aluminum foil, or cardboard boxes to be wasted. The lettuce went into the net bag Carl had along, the spaghetti was weighed and wrapped in a piece of lightweight cardboard with the ends tucked in, and the hamburger was made before our eyes. The butcher weighed the meat, chopped it in pieces, put

Whenever I glanced up, I could see that mysterious pyramid shaped minaret tower beckoning us on.

118

it through a grinder, and wrapped it in paper. The bread had a tiny square of tissue paper around its middle where you could take hold of it to carry it, but was unwrapped otherwise.

I wanted to pay for at least some of the food. "I've got some money left," I said. "I know it won't pay for much, but you might as well have it. And then you better figure out how much I owe you. I can have my parents send it to you. There's the vet assistant's trip, the visit to the doctor, gas for the car, and all the food I've eaten."

But Carl refused my money. "You'd better keep what you have. We don't know yet whether you'll have to pay any more for your ticket from here."

"Will you be sure to let us know how much extra you spent?"

"School and my term of service will be over the end of June. That's only a couple of months away. How about if I stop in Indiana to see you on my way to Kansas? Then I can get a little return hospitality and settle up with your parents—if there's any settling up to do."

"Oh, that would be great! My folks are always glad to see someone who's just come from Algeria. And they'll be especially glad to see you—when they know how much you helped me."

Then, without warning, our evening plans were interrupted. In fact, we never even got to fix the spaghetti and tossed salad or to taste the melon.

When we arrived back at the apartment building, a man standing by the outer doorway stepped forward to meet us.

120

I couldn't understand what the man was saying to Carl. Then Carl explained, "I'm not sure what's going on, Zina, but we're being asked to go at once with him to see the security police."

My heart flip-flopped. "Both of us?"

"Yes. They have both our names on the summons."

"Are we going to be expelled?"

"I have no idea. It may be just for questioning."

As we followed the man, I didn't look around me as eagerly as before. The streets which had been so interesting now seemed frightening and sinister.

When we arrived at the headquarters we were immediately taken into a small office. The two policemen who talked to us there did not wear uniforms. They were probably some kind of secret police. I noticed the one was dressed in dark blue pants and light blue shirt. But it was useless to wonder whether he was the one I thought had followed Lil and me. I had never seen his face that clearly. But I was convinced he was. I felt like asking him if he didn't have any other clothes. Or was blue maybe his favorite color. But of course I was scared stiff and didn't say anything.

He was the one who began to ask me all kinds of questions. He wanted to know where I was born, why I had come back to Algeria, why I had been at the Palmeraie, why I had been with Lil. I answered truthfully, in a shaky voice. But I could tell that my answers didn't impress him. (This was all in French, and Carl was translating for me.)

With Carl it was more of the same. Why had he come to Algeria? Why had he gone to Constantine to visit Lil? Why had he taken me secretly (his word) across the desert?

It seemed as though he was trying to turn everything we'd done into some kind of spying scheme. But then we found out he asked the questions only to try to confirm what they had already made up their minds about. We knew this because, at the end of the questioning, he pulled out of a drawer an already-prepared paper which ordered us to leave the country immediately.

By then I thought I didn't really care. If they didn't want me, I was glad to leave. It would be a relief to get away from being watched all the time. But Carl looked worried. I wondered why. Was it because he had souvenirs and other things he would hate to lose? But it wasn't that.

"We can't leave immediately!" he burst out. "We will leave, of course, if that's what you want. But we can't go until we receive the report from Institut Pasteur about Zina's dog bite."

And then Carl told them about what had happened in El Oued.

"That's a likely story," the other man responded.

"Show them, Zina. Show them where you were bitten."

I stuck out my leg and carefully peeled back the bandage. The wound wasn't so sore anymore and was starting to heal. Maybe they would think it was just a cut of some kind. Still, if they had really been watching us, they should know that Carl's story was true.

"This expulsion order has come from our headquarters in Algiers," the first man said, "and it must be followed."

"If you don't believe me or don't realize the seriousness of rabies, you can call Institut Pasteur," Carl suggested. "Find out if we're telling the truth. Find out whether they have the test results yet. If they do, once we know them, we can leave. If they don't, it should be only the matter of a day or two, and we'll leave then."

The two secret police looked at each other.

"I will call," blue shirt said. "If your story is true and the report is not ready, I will still need to check with Algiers before allowing you to stay longer."

I waited uneasily while he began the process of making the call. What would they do if the tests weren't completed? Would they make us leave anyway?

Carl smiled at me reassuringly, but when he started to say something to me, the other man told him we weren't allowed to talk to each other.

The call was in Arabic, and Carl told me later that he was worried about that, thinking that they could tell us the opposite of what was said on the phone, and we wouldn't know the difference. But when he hung up and gave us the message, we knew that he was telling us truthfully what he had heard.

"The tests have been completed, and they have just sent the results to you and to the people at El Oued," the man said.

He glanced at the paper where he had been making notes during the phone conversation. "The results were positive for rabies," he continued. "That is, the mice which were injected with the dog's brain tissue all died of rabies. And you are recommended to begin the series of injections at once."

I didn't know whether to feel glad or sad. It was good to know rather than to keep wondering. But I certainly wasn't looking forward to the shots.

Carl said he would need a prescription from somewhere to get the serum, that we couldn't leave without it, and that I should have the first shot before we left.

"I will take care of that," the first man said. "You are not free to wander around the city."

So he wrote a note and sent a policeman with it to the pharmacy, and ordered him to find a nurse to come along and give me the first shot.

When the policeman had gone, Carl said, "Since we need to wait, couldn't we go get our suitcases ready to take along? It won't take much time. You can send someone along to guard us."

That required some thinking over. At last Carl was given permission to go. Accompanied by an officer, he left for his apartment to bring back a suitcase for each of us.

In the meantime, there I sat alone, waiting. Confused thoughts were whirling through my mind. I wasn't sure how I felt. In a way I was excited about being expelled. What a story I'd have to tell back home! Much more exciting than only having come to Algeria for a visit and then having returned.

But at the same time I felt a little angry at myself for liking being expelled so I'd have a story to tell. Mixed in with that, I was angry at Algeria, at the way people were not free to worship and believe as they wanted to, at the way people could be sent out of the country for no real reason.

Mostly, though, I felt sad. I thought of the beautiful countryside—the snowy mountains, the crested dunes, the precipices of Constantine, the blue sea. I thought of the unusual things I'd seen—the haughty camels and their nomad owners going north, the tattooed woman who'd given me the pitcher, the wedding celebration with its music and dancing, the hidden oasis farm, and yes, even the dog. I was sad because I'd loved most of what I'd seen of my native land and its people, and I knew that once I left, I would never see it or them again.

I looked at my palm. The orange-brown color of the henna was beginning to fade. It made me sad to think that the memory of what I'd seen and experienced would fade, too.

However, you see that I found a way to prevent

that. By writing down my story, my memories will never disappear like the henna did. I can always come and read what I have written, and in the story, Algeria will come alive to me again.

* * *

P.S. Before long they were back with the suitcases, the serum, and the nurse. That first shot into my lower abdomen, and the others later, were not fun. But neither were they as bad as I had expected. Then the policemen hauled us to the airport, and put us on the first plane going north, the first stage of our journey home.

Author's note:
This story is fiction, and all the persons in it are fictional. Two of the incidents, however, are true. The raid on the Palmeraie did happen in December 1969, and an American girl who was asleep missed being taken with the others. The dog-bite incident is also true. It happened to me, but not in El Oued, and the dog's head was sent by train rather than by plane. (But the mice did die, and I needed to take the fourteen shots.)

All the places described are real, as are the problems faced by both foreign and Algerian Christians.

Marian Hostetler served in Algeria nine years under the Mennonite Board of Missions. She taught primary school subjects in French, sewing in the homes, English as a foreign language in a boys' high school, and worked as a secretary-librarian in the Christian Center for North African studies.

She knows firsthand the frustrations of foreign Christians who try to live the way of Christ in a Muslim land and what it means for Algerians to be Christians.

Other overseas experiences of Marian (an Orrville, Ohio, native) include travel in Europe, Scandinavia, and Israel; participation in a work camp in Austria; a year of study in Paris; a summer of mission/service work in Chad, and more recently a summer in Nepal.

Presently Marian teaches third grade at Concord West Side School, Elkhart, Indiana. She received her MS degree in elementary education from Indiana University, Bloomington, Indiana; her BA from Goshen College, Goshen, Indiana; and has also studied at Goshen Biblical Seminary, Goshen, Indiana.

She is the author of *African Adventure* and *Journey to Jerusalem*, also published by Herald Press, a quarter of Grade 3 and 4 of The Foundation Series Sunday School curriculum, and articles and stories in *Purpose* and *Story Friends*.

Marian enjoys reading and painting, as well as writing. She is an active member of Belmont Mennonite Church in Elkhart.